THE
INTENTION
JOURNAL

The powerful, research-backed planner
for achieving your big investing goals
in just ninety days.

BRANDON TURNER

BiggerPockets®
PUBLISHING

DENVER, COLORADO

The Intention Journal
Brandon Turner

Published by BiggerPockets Publishing LLC, Denver, CO
Copyright © 2019 by Brandon Turner.
All Rights Reserved.

Published in the United States of America
10 9 8 7 6 5 4 3 2 1

This journal belongs to ...

_____

_____

_____

WAIT!

Before starting, visit the link below to learn
how to get the most out of this journal, as well as how to join
an Intentional Mastermind Group!

www.BiggerPockets.com/start
Access Code: INTENTION

WELCOME TO THE INTENTION JOURNAL

I had never been more terrified in my life.

I was clinging to the side of a 1,000-pound horse as it tried to buck me from its back, gripping whatever piece of hair or leather I could get my hands on. Secretly, I just hoped I wouldn't fall off and die. Turns out that half of my prayer was answered—I'm still here! But I did fall, landing directly under the large, angry horse. My helmet, along with my pre-teen ego, was crushed to pieces.

Let's back up: It had been my first time horseback riding, so naturally the summer camp counselor gave me the largest, meanest-looking horse in the bunch on that hot July afternoon. After a solid 90 seconds of instruction, they placed me on the animal and told me to just ride around the corral a bit. "It's easy," they said. And the first several minutes were fine and easy; I was even beginning to enjoy myself as I smiled like an idiot ear to ear, waving to my friends on the other side of the fence.

We graduated from the fenced corral to a trail ride and, as we neared the woods, a deer noticed us and sprinted away, spooking the beast I was unfortunately hitching a ride on. The horse, instinctively, bolted—like a cat out of a bathtub—and I found myself clinging to the horse's back as it bucked and galloped with fear.

I'd like to say I did what any tobacco-chewing, gun-toting cowboy would have done: grabbed the reins, pulled back gently, and calmed the horse down into a peaceful walk, nodding handsomely to the pretty girls—just another day as an outlaw on the frontier. But I was 12 and scared out of my mind, so I just clung to the horse's neck and held on for dear life as it took me on this wild ride. I lasted 30 seconds on the horse, which felt like 30 minutes, before I finally tipped off the left side and landed directly under the horse's back leg. If it weren't for that helmet, I would have been crushed by his hoof.

For those of you who know how to ride a horse, you likely found amusement from this story, knowing how easily I could have calmed the horse by simply using the reins. Those reins are connected to a tiny little "bit" inside the horse's mouth. Pull left, the horse veers left. Pull right, the horse veers right. Pull back, the horse slows down, then comes to a halt. (It doesn't hurt to say "Whooooa!" as you pull back.) That 1,000 pound Goliath-of-an-animal can be controlled by a 2-pound piece of metal and some strips of leather.

Incredible, isn't it?

Most people go through life the way that I rode that horse: clinging on for dear life. You may not know where you are headed. You may not know why you are going in a certain direction. And you may not always happy about the journey.

Little do you know the power you hold in your hands.

When life spooks you and throws you into an uproar, you hold on tighter, hoping the shaking ceases, never understanding that you can control the creature you ride. No, you can't control what the beast will always do, but a gentle pull in the right direction is all that's needed to get back on track.

This journal is meant to be the "bit" on your life's journey. Though it takes less than 10 minutes to fill out each day, this journal will ensure that you are the one directing the powerful animal upon which you ride, and give you control of something you thought uncontrollable.

The Foundation Upon Which Success Is Built

I'm sure somewhere in the back of your mind you have an idea of where you want your life to take you. But do you live intentionally to achieve that end? Do your daily actions line up with that destination? How do you even know you're doing the right things to get you there?

This journal is meant to help you get on the right path toward your ultimate goal on a daily basis. In short, this journal will help you live intentionally.

That's what *The Intention Journal* is all about. It will help you define who you are going to become rather than waiting to see what fate has in store. It's about controlling the beast. It's about intention. It's time to stop thinking of your life as something that happens to you. It's time to take the reins of your life and begin the most fantastic ride you'll ever experience.

Intention is the foundation upon which great success is built.

Want a great marriage? Be *intentional* about it!

Want an early retirement? Be *intentional* about it!

Want to move to Maui to surf? Be *intentional* about it!

Being intentional means no longer living life as it comes; it means living *proactively* rather than reactively. It means taking control of the God-given freedom we have to make choices.

Think about it for a moment. In the past 24 hours, how many minutes did you actually spend living proactively? If you are like most people, those moments of intention are few and far in-between. But what would happen if you spent more time being intentional about your day and your time?

A Simple Formula for Success

But what exactly is *intention*?

For the purposes of this journal, I want to slightly redefine the term. Perhaps you've uttered the words, "*I had every intention to...*" when you're about to make an excuse for why you didn't accomplish something. But, frankly, there is a wide chasm between desire and intention. Desire is "I want that." Intention is "I'm committed to that."

Webster's Dictionary defines intention as "a determination to act in a certain way." Read that again—slowly:

Intention is "a determination to act in a certain way."

Now that you've read it again, did you notice that it doesn't define intention as, "a determination to *get somewhere*" or "a goal to *be something*"? It's not about the end result, about hoping to get some goal accomplished. It's about the way you act.

The key difference between desire and commitment is *action*.

Imagine this: Your best friend is sitting across the dinner table from you at your favorite restaurant. Your friend looks at you and says, "I'm going to get in the best shape of my life this year. I'm going to get that six-pack I've wanted. I'm going to look incredible. I'm going to be intentional about transforming my body." And as they finish this exclamation, they look up to the server who just arrived and boldly order a jumbo triple-decker greasy burger, a side of fries, a milkshake, and four sugary alcoholic drinks throughout the course of the evening. The food comes and you watch, in disbelief, as your friend consumes every calorie with a smile on their face.

Now tell me: Was this friend truly *intentional* about their decision to get into the best shape of their life? Or did they simply *desire* the outcome?

Michael Jordan, the star of the 1996 classic *Space Jam* (Oh, I think he also played some basketball...) once said, "*Some people want it to happen, some wish it would happen, others make it happen.*" This journal is designed to help you get from "want" to "make."

Therefore, when you think about the concept of "intention" I want to introduce a simple formula, called *The Intention Formula*:

Goals + Commitment + Action = Intention

To be intentional, you need to know where you are going. You also need to be committed to that result. And you must take the correct actions needed to get there. Without all three parts of the *The Intention Formula*, your life is left hanging to the side of that horse, hoping it just happens to take you to the right place.

This journal is your roadmap, your framework for following the above formula. It's a way to detail a few important goals, commit to them, and actually carry out the actions needed to achieve the level of success you desire.

What Most People Get Wrong About Success

Success is not a feeling, a plan, or a wish. Success is brought about by the small, often repetitive actions taken every day. The hours in the gym. The phone calls made. The books read. There's no fanfare. No ticker tape parade. No trophies. Success is brought about by taking the necessary, deliberate action until your goal is achieved. Therefore, for those who can identify what the right daily actions are (and have a system for ensuring they get accomplished), success is generous to show up larger than imaginable!

And that's why *The Intention Journal* was created: to help you identify those small actions and ensure they get done—each day—so you can reach your highest potential.

Isn't it time you had the business you want, the physical health you desire, the relationships you seek, the financial freedom you long for? Isn't it time to stop wishing, stop wanting, and start making those things happen?

If you're ready for the most intense 90 days of your life—90 days of pure intention—then it's time to make a change. Jim Rohn said it best when he famously quipped, "Life doesn't get better by chance, it gets better by change." This journal will change your life if you follow the plan. Not in the foo-foo, pie-in-the-sky way the "change your life" phrase is normally uttered, but by literally changing the actions you take each and every day. You'll line up your goals, commitments, and actions to create an undefeatable freight train of momentum that will carry you into the future—a future that you can look forward to.

A future built on intention.

My Obsession

Why do some individuals achieve incredible success—leading to a life of great health, happiness, and financial independence—yet so many others struggle, fail, and give up on their dreams?

I'm Brandon Turner: business owner, real estate investor, podcaster, surfer, husband, father, bestselling author, and creator of *The Intention Journal* from BiggerPockets. For the past decade I've been obsessed with the question of why:

- Why do a small number of people succeed and most fail?
- Why do some people look and feel fantastic, while most of America is overweight?
- Why do some businesses make incredible profits where others fizzle out?
- Why do some marriages last a lifetime, and others cycle through spouses more frequently than the car they drive?

More importantly, I tried to answer the question to address my own shortcomings. Why wasn't I succeeding to the levels of those around me?

As I was building my business, I found myself continually struggling to keep up. Always reacting, always struggling, always playing catch up. My finances suffered. My relationships were rocky. My body was far from ideal. I worked 100 hours a week and felt like I was barely making progress on anything. I had too many goals, too little time, and no clear way to get the life I wanted.

Maybe you can relate?

But then something changed: I changed. I became intentional about the kind of life I wanted to live. How I wanted my business to be. How I wanted to physically look and feel. How I wanted to interact with friends, family, coworkers, and others. And over time, my intentions led to actions which led to real, lasting change.

Today I earn more income than I spend from passive investments. I get to help millions of people each month get closer to their financial goals through the podcasts, books, and blog posts I've created. I live in my dream home in my dream location—surfing, jogging, hiking, and living an idyllic life in the Hawaiian sun. I work fewer hours, spend more time with my wife and daughter, and have time to sit back and watch the whales breach in front of the golden sunset every night. I truly am in the best shape of my life. And it was largely made possible because I became intentional about it. It wasn't because I became intentional about the outcome, but I began to follow *The Intention Formula*. I knew where I wanted to go. I made true commitments toward getting there. And I took the daily action needed to pull it off.

But this journal is not about me. This journal, from here on out, is about you. It's about your future. About your legacy. About your health. Your finances. Your relationships.

This is your story.

A Scientific Case for Success

As I mentioned a moment ago, I've been obsessed with the concept of what separates successful achievers from those who give up, fail, or never get started. Maybe you recognize that question from *The BiggerPockets Podcast* because we've asked it to hundreds of guests over the past six years. And throughout this time, we've seen certain patterns emerge from the inspiring stories of those who have found incredible success.

But, of course, causation doesn't always equal correlation. Do the daily habits, tactics, and routines of these highly successful people actually contribute to their success? Or is a byproduct of their already successful nature? For that, I turned to the world of cognitive science and psychology, spending hundreds of hours poring over books, published research papers, and in-depth studies of human behavior to find not only what seems to make people successful, but what also *actually* makes people successful.

After years of study, the journal you hold in your hands is the result.

It combines the best practices of top performers worldwide, as backed by the newest research into human potential. It's designed to help you create and track high-level, 90-day goals, establish weekly objectives needed to stay on track, define your most important next step for each objective, give you space for an end-of-day (and end-of-week) reflection on your progress, help you build positive daily habits, and much, much more.

In other words: This book is going to help you accomplish your dreams in just a few minutes of daily, intentional journaling. Consider this journal your roadmap to the person you are about to become. Each day you'll identify and take the right steps to reach your biggest goals, no matter how far away they seem.

It's time to live a life of intention, starting with the next 90 days.

And we'll be here for you the whole time.

INTRODUCTION PART II

HOW TO USE THIS JOURNAL

Chance didn't bring you to this journal.

Chance didn't encourage you to open it.

And chance isn't going transform the next 90 days of your life.

Intention will.

Whether you know it or not, the mere act of picking up this journal was a lesson in intentionality. You desire something better from your life, and you believe (as I do) that this journal will help you achieve it. So...you've already begun. Congratulations!

But before we get any further, it's time to walk you through how this journal is going to work. I know it's tempting to just jump in and begin, but let's take a few minutes to understand the why behind each section of this journal, along with how to fill it out to maximize your success.

How the Next 90 Days Look

The Intention Journal is designed to help you break your big goals down into the smallest parts, which increases your odds of accomplishing the big goal.

Wait…that's wrong, isn't it?

In reality, it's not about increasing your odds. This isn't chance. This isn't hope. This is intention. In fact, this journal is designed to break your big goals down into the smallest parts, which increases your ability to make your dreams come true.

There. That sounds better!

We need to get rid of the idea that success is something that happens to us. Instead, let's consider success a direct result of our day-to-day actions. This journal is about taking big goals—which you will create in Part II—and working backwards to determine what those daily actions are. Then, you'll schedule them throughout your week and your day to move quickly and effectively toward the life you desire.

To do this, your journal contains two regularly updated sections:

The Weekly Battle Plan—The Weekly Battle Plan is a weekly strategy session designed to lift you out of the everyday muck, so you can survey your life like a general overseeing the battlefield. It's a place to work on your life, rather than in your life. This weekly section is imperative to an intentional life, as it will define the steps you take each day. I recommend completing this session at the start of each week (Sunday night or Monday morning) to launch you like a rocket into the next seven days. During this time, you'll write down your goals and a specific, tangible objective for the coming week, as well as the motivation for your objective and the roadblocks that could prevent you from reaching your goal.

The Weekly Battle Plan is also where you'll track and develop weekly habits. Want to read more? Track it. Want to analyze more deals? Track it. Want to deepen your relationship with your spouse? Track your date nights!

Finally, the Weekly Battle Plan includes an end-of-week review so you can reflect. This section should take between 15–30 minutes to complete—but look at this time more as an "investment" than "time spent" because, due to the nature of intentional planning, you will save many otherwise wasted hours.

The Daily Action Plan—The Daily Action Plan is where you get in the trenches and fight. Each morning, you'll write down the three goals you previously established, as well as the weekly objectives you defined during your Weekly Battle Plan, to place yourself in the right mindset for the day. You'll also identify your Most Important Next Step (M.I.N.S.), which is the large, actionable task you can do toward accomplishing your goal. (More on that in the introduction video at www.BiggerPockets.com/start.) And you'll have room to track your business funnel, which I'll explain more about in a moment.

Finally, you'll time block your day, scheduling each moment so you run your day, rather than your day running you. The Daily Action Plan ends with an evening review, encouraging you to spend a few moments each night reflecting on the day to see what worked, what didn't, and what you can improve upon in the future.

The Weekly Battle Plan and The Daily Action Plan are your two greatest weapons in the battle for intention. Use them to transform your life over the next 90 days. By taking time each week and day to be intentional, you'll achieve amazing results: more free time, less stress, and new control over your life. That's the power of living intentionally.

Your Business Funnel

The Daily Action Plan also contains a diagram of a funnel. Although a funnel doesn't work for every goal, chances are, at least one of your goals can be tracked inside a funnel—especially if the goal is related to business. The concept of a funnel is simple: a lot of "input" is put into the top, and only a small "outcome" is produced from the bottom. For example, perhaps you work in sales and one of your goals is to increase your sales. So, you might find that:

If you make 100 phone calls,
you might actually speak to 30 individuals,
and sell three products,
at a profit of $50 each,
netting you $150 in profit.

Or perhaps you, like myself, are working toward buying real estate deals. Your funnel might look more like this:

100 property leads obtained
30 properties analyzed
5 offers made
1 offer accepted

Or maybe your goal is to hire a new assistant, your funnel might be:

Received 20 applicants
Interviewed 5 prospects
Offered 1 person the job

Regardless of what your funnel is designed to accomplish, funnels help you visualize goals and demonstrate that results don't happen in a vacuum. In other words, if you want more sales, set goals and increase certain levels of the funnel. Let's look at the first example above—the sales call to sell the $50 product. If you wanted to double your income, you could find ways to increase the success of each part of the funnel. For example:

100 phone calls	150 phone calls
30 conversations	60 conversations
(30% of calls answered)	(40% of calls answered)
3 sales (10% of conversations sold)	8 sales (13% of conversations sold)
$50 each (profit per sale)	$50 each (profit per sale)
$150 total profit ($50 x 3)	$400 total profit ($50 x 8)

Notice in the above example, small adjustments to each level of the funnel produced a massive increase in profit at the end. Funnels are the key to most business success, and top business-owners view their company through the lens of a funnel. They constantly ask, "How do we increase total profit by making small improvements to the funnel?" This "how" question leads to answers. And answers lead to greater profit.

The beauty of thinking in terms of funnels is twofold:

1. You realize you don't need a miracle to increase your outcome. Small changes are easy to obtain quickly and can usually be achieved with minor tweaks, split testing, and innovative ideas. Trying to figure out how to double traffic on a website in the next 30 days, legally and sustainably, is next to impossible. Trying to figure out how to produce a 10 percent increase across three levels of the funnel? Now, that's doable.

2. Funnels give you specific goals to fight for. I believe one of the most powerful words in the English language is "HOW." I talk a lot about the idea of switching your "I can't" vocabulary to the simple question, "How can I?" When you think in terms of funnels, each step becomes a "How can I?" puzzle:
- How can I make 150 phone calls instead of 100?
- How can I get 40 percent of my calls answered instead of 30 percent?
- How can I get 12 percent of people to buy instead of 10 percent?

Suddenly, your business becomes a game or a code that can be cracked. You can achieve these numbers when you focus. Put your whole mind, and your team's mind, to setting goals and achieving each goal in your funnel.

I call this the "If-If-If-Then Game." If you can achieve your goal in step one, if you can achieve it in step two, and if you can achieve it in the other steps, then you will hit your revenue goals at the bottom of the funnel, guaranteed.

It's so simple, yet so powerful. Therefore, The Intention Journal includes room each and every day to track a funnel. If you have business goals, my guess is you have a funnel to track, and through tracking you will tend to improve that funnel.

INTRODUCTION PART III
THREE BIG GOALS

Research shows that having too many goals can be detrimental to accomplishing any of them. On the other hand, setting too few goals means not living up to your full potential.

That's why *The Intention Journal* has space for **three big goals**. These can be whatever you want, but I'd encourage you to make only one goal in each category. Maybe one is a business goal (for example, to buy a real estate investment property), one could be a fitness goal (maybe to lose a certain number of pounds), and perhaps one could be a relationship goal (such as spending more time with your children, away from your phone).

Each week, you'll write down your goals in the Weekly Battle Plan and once again in the Daily Action Plan. This may seem repetitive, but regularly reviewing your goals maximizes your focus to achieve them.

However, you need to set your goals before you can review them each day. Let's do that now!

To outline this section, I'm going to turn to an acronym that, although overused in the personal development space, just makes too much sense to ignore here. That acronym is "SMART," and the five tips that make up this acronym can help you create the most powerful goals possible.

SMART stands for:

Specific
Measurable
Attainable
Relevant
Time-Bound

Over the rest of this chapter, we're going to spend a few moments on each of these areas, making sure your goals are SMART enough to change your life. Let's begin.

Specific
Vague goals are nothing but wishes. If you want to make a wish, go throw a penny in a fountain. But if you want to set a goal that you know you will achieve—it needs to be specific.

Why do specific goals matter? Because without a specific destination, it is nearly impossible to arrive there. "I want to be rich" is a great wish, but what does that mean? How much is rich? Is having $1 million rich? And if so, do you mean $1 million in equity rich or does it have to be cash in the bank? The more specific you can make your goal, the easier you'll have turning that goal into a reality. Therefore, define your goal specifically—and then write it down (which you'll do in a moment).

Writing down your goals can serve several purposes. First, a written goal is not easily forgotten. By writing your goal down, and keeping it somewhere conspicuous, the goal is consistently on the top of your mind. Second, a written goal is a great way to convince your mind that you are serious about being committed. It's one thing to think "I want to raise my credit score by 20 points" and another thing entirely to write that goal down. If you truly are committed to achieving your goal—take the few seconds required and write it down!

Measurable

Is your goal something that can be measured? If not, it's going to be quite difficult to know you've reached it—and even more difficult to create benchmarks to monitor how close or far away you are from achieving your goal. For example, setting a goal that says "I want to work harder" is not measurable in that format. What does that even mean? Are we talking about increasing the number of hours worked, eliminating the number of distractions that interrupt oneself during work, or something entirely different?

Instead, make sure your goal can be measured and/or quantified. How many rental houses do you want to own? How much cash do you want to have in the bank? How much can you improve your credit score? These are all examples of a measurable goal.

Attainable

Now, we have to be careful with this one. "Attainable" has become synonymous with "safe" or "reasonable." It's been changed to mean "easy to obtain" rather than its true definition of "what's possible when stretched." The key word there is "stretched."

Imagine a child trying to reach a cookie jar on a high shelf. There is a big difference between "easy to reach," "stretch," and "impossible" for children. The bottom shelf, where most people metaphorically place their goals, requires very little effort to get to. But, on the other hand, the highest shelf will never happen no matter how hard the child might try. The middle shelf, though, might require some tippy-toes or maybe even a stool. And here, where stretching a little to reach victory, is where you want to place your goals.

The problem with setting small, easy-to-reach goals is that they promote small, easy thinking. An easy goal fails to kick your mind into overdrive, allowing it to drift along on cruise control indefinitely.

Of course, a larger goal requires a whole different set of plans. When you increase the size of your goal, your entire mindset is forced to shift and think of the problem differently—to think bigger, smarter, and with more efficiency.

For example, let's say your goal was to buy one rental house per year. You have to start by looking at a few deals, making a few offers, and then boom—you've got a deal. But what if you raised your goal to 10 houses? or 20? Or 30? This kind of goal requires entirely different thinking. You might need to hire a team, an assistant, or find a better real estate agent. Maybe it means you should shift to buying multifamily properties so you can reach your goal in one big purchase!

In setting your goal, don't make it laughably impossible, but you should reach and stretch for something a bit greater than you think you can accomplish. Trust me, the stretching will be great for your soul, your body, and your business.

Relevant

Does your current goal relate to the ultimate goal of your life? In other words, does your goal get you to where (or who) you ultimately want to be? If not, it's time to reconsider your goal. Your goal should support that purpose, not detract from it. But all too often it's easy to pick a goal because it sounds cool or popular, even if it doesn't support where you are headed in life. I've often stated my goal as a real estate investor is to own 1,000 rental units within three years. But what if 1,000 rental units isn't what you need to live the life you want? Maybe that sounds like a nightmare to you! Be sure that your goals are relevant to your vision, not someone else's.

In addition, a goal can take years to achieve, and the journey to achieve that goal is often not worth the goal itself. Most of your life will be spent working to achieve your goals, so make sure the journey is relevant to your purpose. Yes, the road to your big goals may not always be perfect, and sacrifice is required. Just be sure that the sacrifice is not greater than the benefit of achieving your goal in the end.

Let's use an example from real estate. Many people choose to invest in real estate because they want the freedom to travel, be home with family, and not have to answer to a boss, and real estate can help you achieve this end. However, many of the investors I know get caught up in the game of "building a bigger and bigger business" and lose sight of their purpose. They end up working 100-plus hours on their business for decades in an effort to get richer. The more they buy, the more they need. In the end, they've lost sight of why they got into real estate in the first place. As poet Thomas Merton said, "People may spend their whole lives climbing the ladder of success only to find, once they reach the top, that the ladder is leaning against the wrong wall."

No one gets to the end of their life and wants their epitaph inscribed with, *"He hustled for 80 years and now he's the richest man in this graveyard."* Remember: Goals are important, but the journey is what we live through day to day. We need to be careful that the goals we set don't turn us down a path that we don't want for too long.

Time-Bound

Finally, a powerful goal should have a deadline. Without a timeline for completion, your goal is bound to be punted year after year, never fully coming to fruition. Deadlines, however, spur us into action. Have you ever noticed how incredibly focused you can get on a project when it's due the next day? We procrastinate and procrastinate and do 90 percent of what we need to get done in the final 10 percent of the time we have allotted for it. Rather than fight this procrastination, use it to your advantage and set short deadlines to achieve your goals. Want to lose 10 pounds? Good. Want to lose 10 pounds in the next 90 days? Well, that is going to require some hustle, which is exactly what a goal is meant to do. When we have a short deadline for our goal, we must think, plan, and act intelligently to achieve the goal within the timeframe.

I previously shared one of my goals to own 1,000 rental units in the next three years. However, I've broken that down to a more time-sensitive number: 200 by the end of this year. Then, I've broken it down even further to define my goal of getting a 50-unit (or greater) property under contract in the next 90 days.

Or maybe your long-term vision is to pay off $100,000 in student loans. If that's the case, perhaps make it a goal to pay $5,000 over the next 90 days. Now your mind can begin to formulate a plan that can achieve that short-term goal, rather than trying to figure out how to pay off $100,000.

It's okay to have a far-off vision for your future, but split up far-reaching goals into shorter sprints.

It's Your Turn

Now it's time to begin writing your goals.

No doubt, in this chapter you've already been formulating what your goals are going to be. But remember: It's not enough to know them. If you truly want to be committed, it's important that you *write your goals down and review them regularly*. Therefore, use the following space to write down the three goals you plan to accomplish over the next 90 days.

Your friend,

Brandon Turner

90-DAY GOAL #1

_____

I will achieve this goal by: _____

I want to achieve this goal because: _____

_____

_____

I will achieve this goal by doing these things: _____

_____

_____

90-DAY GOAL #2

_____

I will achieve this goal by: _____

I want to achieve this goal because: _____

_____

_____

I will achieve this goal by doing these things: _____

_____

_____

90-DAY GOAL #3

_____

I will achieve this goal by: _____

I want to achieve this goal because: _____

_____

_____

I will achieve this goal by doing these things: _____

_____

_____

The following pages contain a sample of what the Weekly Battle Plan and Daily Action Plan might look like. Feel free to use these as inspiration or ignore them and chart your own path.

This is your book. Start writing it!

WEEKLY BATTLE PLANNING

Week of __November 1st - November 6th__

GOAL REVIEW AND WEEKLY OBJECTIVES

Each week, review your big goals and subsequently break those goals down into objectives, determine the source of your motivation, identify potential roadblocks, and time-block those activities.

GOAL #1 __Buy a single family rental property in Cincinnati by Dec 31st__

I want this goal because __I want financial freedom to spend more time with my kids__

This week, my objective is __Send out 400 direct mail letters__

In pursuit of this objective, the largest roadblock might be __I might not have the time to print all 400 letters__

...and I'll overcome that roadblock by __I'll hire my sister-in-law to print all the direct mail letters__

I will work on this goal on __Tuesday at 3 pm__
(day/time)   (Now, go schedule this on your calendar.)

GOAL #2 __Lose 20 lbs by December 1st__

I want this goal because __I want to live to see my great-grandkids, and look good for my wife!__

This week, my objective is __Lose 2 pounds__

In pursuit of this objective, the largest roadblock might be __I might get too busy to work out or cook__

...and I'll overcome that roadblock by __putting workouts on my calendar and planning meals for the week__

I will work on this goal on __M, W, & F at 6:30 am__
(day/time)   (Now, go schedule this on your calendar.)

GOAL #3 __Find a real estate mentor__

I want this goal because __I want financial freedom - but I know I'll need help. A mentor can help!__

This week, my objective is __Attend one local real estate meetup__

In pursuit of this objective, the largest roadblock might be __I might be too nervous to attend an event__

...and I'll overcome that roadblock by __Asking a friend to come with me__

I will work on this goal on __Friday at 7pm__
(day/time)   (Now, go schedule this on your calendar.)

> **The #1 Most Important Thing to move my goals forward this week...** | Send the direct mail letters. I HAVE to do this!

(Now, go schedule this on your calendar.)

BUILDING AND TRACKING DAILY HABITS

Use the following chart to identify three to six key habits or processes that, when carried out consistently, will result in positive changes and help you achieve your goals. In the first column, identify the habit; in the second, set a goal for the number of times you wish to accomplish this; and then track your progress throughout the week.

Habit/Process	Goal	SUNDAY	MONDAY	TUESDAY	WEDNESDAY	THURSDAY	FRIDAY	SATURDAY	Total
Analyze a deal	5	0	2	0	3	1	0	0	6!
Review my goals	7	x	x		x	x	x		5
Exercise 30 mins	3	x		x		x			3
Eat 2,000 cal	5	x	x		x	x	x		6!
Read 30 mins	4	x	x				x	x	3
Listen to BP podcast	2		x			x			2

END OF WEEK REVIEW

Looking at your wins and losses from your recent past can help you identify patterns, celebrate wins, determine course corrections, and ultimately lead you closer to your destination.

How did I get closer to my goals this week? **I sent out the direct mail letters!**

What lessons did I learn this week that will help me next week? **I don't need to reinvent the wheel.**
I can just find out what works for other people, in similar markets, and do the same. It worked this week!

On a scale of 1–10, with 10 being the highest, I would rate last week's productivity at a **7**

Last week I studied...
"How to Invest in Real Estate"

Next week I'll study...
"...Managing Rental Properties"

This week, did I...	Yes	No
take care of my body and mind?	X	
take care of my relationships?	X	
take enough breaks?		X
make time for myself?		X
get enough sleep?		X

Did I accomplish my #1 most important goal last week?	**YES!**	If yes, celebrate! If not, why?	**Whoop whoop!**

SAMPLE DAILY PAGE LEFT

JAN | FEB | MAR | APR | MAY | JUN | JUL | AUG | SEP | OCT | NOV | DEC
1 2 3 4 5 6 7 8 9 10 11 12 13 14 15 16 17 18 19 20 21 22 23 24 25 26 27 28 29 30 31

DAILY ACTION PLAN
MORNING ROUTINE

Hours Slept __8 hrs.__   Wake-up Time __6 am__

Water [X] Exercise [X] Daily Journal [X] breakfast [X] meditation [X]

This morning, I'm grateful for __the strong friendships I have with John and Jim__

GOALS AND M.I.N.S.

Goals are important to review daily, reinforcing your objectives to your conscious and subconscious mind. But goals alone are not enough. It's also vital that you take time to identify your Most Important Next Step (M.I.N.S.) for each goal, so your goal transforms into an action. And remember, when it comes to M.I.N.S., be specific.

GOAL #1 __Buy a single family rental house by Dec 31st__

Weekly Objective: __Send out 400 direct mail letters__

M.I.N.S. __Call my sister-in-law and ask her to print these and mail them by Friday__

GOAL #2 __Lose 20 lbs__

Weekly Objective: __Lose 2 lbs__

M.I.N.S. __Lay out my running shoes the night before and put my running shoes on my feet at 6:30am__

GOAL #3 __Find a real estate mentor__

Weekly Objective: __Attend a local real estate event__

M.I.N.S. __Go to BiggerPockets.com/events and register for the local meetup - then call John__

I can consider today a "win" if I...

Get the direct mail campaign out of my hands!

This is your #1 Most Important Thing!

	GOAL		REALITY
		Calls Made	
	400		450!
		Appointments	
	5		6!
	0 offers this week	Sales	0
		$	
	0 this week		0

SAMPLE DAILY PAGE RIGHT

TODAY'S TIME-BLOCKING ACTIVITIES

High-achievers know that what gets scheduled gets done. Take a few minutes to think about your goals, your M.I.N.S., and schedule your day. Don't forget to include several breaks.

5:00	11:00 break at 11:15am	5:00 Family time
5:30 wake up by 6am	11:30 WORK	5:30 Family time
6:00 jog 30 mins	12:00 Call sister-in-law about direct mail	6:00 Family time
6:30 shower/hair/ family breakfast, etc.	12:30 Lunch	6:30 Dinner
7:00 read	1:00 WORK	7:00 Family time
7:30 leave for work	1:30 WORK	7:30 Family time
8:00 WORK	2:00 WORK	8:00 Analyze one property
8:30 WORK	2:30 break	8:30 with BP Calculators
9:00 WORK	3:00 WORK	9:00 TV with wife
9:30 break	3:30 WORK	9:30 TV with wife
10:00 WORK	4:00 drive home	10:00 lights out
10:30 WORK	4:30	10:30

☒ Did I include enough breaks in the day?

☒ Did I schedule my #1 Most Important Thing?

EVENING REVIEW

Did you accomplish your #1 Most Important Thing today? Yes ☒ No ☐

Today was awesome because __I did my morning workout and I got my sister-in-law started on the direct mail campaign.__

Today I struggled with __Although I planned on family time from 5-8pm, I ended up on a work call for 45 minutes of that time. I need to set better boundaries with work/home life.__

On a scale of 1–10, with 10 being the highest, I would rate today's productivity at a __8__

Tomorrow I will...
- jog four miles in the AM
- call John about the RE meetup
- stretch for twenty minutes

Notes

$250,000	$175,000
x.7	-$35,000
$175,000	$140,000

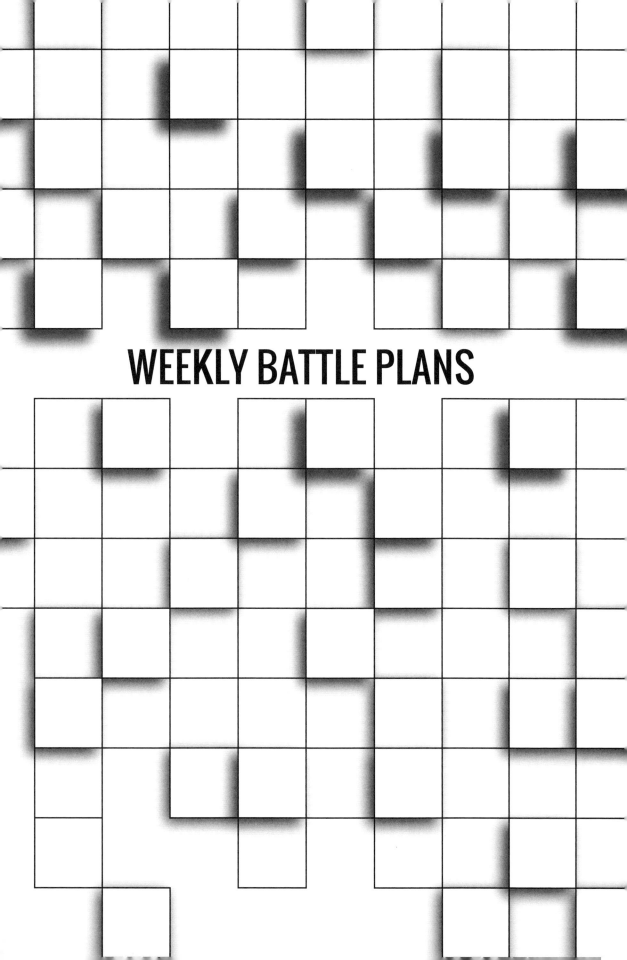

WEEKLY BATTLE PLANS

WEEKLY BATTLE PLANNING

Week of _____

GOAL REVIEW AND WEEKLY OBJECTIVES

Each week, review your big goals and subsequently break those goals down into objectives, determine the source of your motivation, identify potential roadblocks, and time-block those activities.

GOAL #1 _____

I want this goal because _____

This week, my objective is _____

In pursuit of this objective, the largest roadblock might be _____

...and I'll overcome that roadblock by _____

I will work on this goal on _____
                                        (day/time)   (Now, go schedule this on your calendar.)

GOAL #2 _____

I want this goal because _____

This week, my objective is _____

In pursuit of this objective, the largest roadblock might be _____

...and I'll overcome that roadblock by _____

I will work on this goal on _____
                                          (day/time)   (Now, go schedule this on your calendar.)

GOAL #3 _____

I want this goal because _____

This week, my objective is _____

In pursuit of this objective, the largest roadblock might be _____

...and I'll overcome that roadblock by _____

I will work on this goal on _____
                                          (day/time)   (Now, go schedule this on your calendar.)

The #1 Most Important Thing to move my goals forward this week...

(Now, go schedule this on your calendar.)

BUILDING AND TRACKING DAILY HABITS

Use the following chart to identify three to six key habits or processes that, when carried out consistently, will result in positive changes and help you achieve your goals. In the first column, identify the habit; in the second, set a goal for the number of times you wish to accomplish this; and then track your progress throughout the week.

Habit/Process	Goal	SUNDAY	MONDAY	TUESDAY	WEDNESDAY	THURSDAY	FRIDAY	SATURDAY	Total

END OF WEEK REVIEW

Looking at your wins and losses from your recent past can help you identify patterns, celebrate wins, determine course corrections, and ultimately lead you closer to your destination.

How did I get closer to my goals this week? _____

_____

What lessons did I learn this week that will help me next week? _____

_____

On a scale of 1–10, with 10 being the highest, I would rate last week's productivity at a _____

Last week I studied...

Next week I'll study...

This week, did I...	Yes	No
take care of my body and mind ?	☐	☐
take care of my relationships?	☐	☐
take enough breaks?	☐	☐
make time for myself?	☐	☐
get enough sleep?	☐	☐

Did I accomplish my #1 most important goal last week?

If yes, celebrate! If not, why?

MY WEEK _____

MON

TUE

WED

THU

FRI

SAT

SUN

BRAIN DUMP

SUCCESS TIP

A Fresh Start

We all know New Year's Day is a popular time to start something new: a new diet, a new fitness plan, or maybe just doing a better job saving money. The new year signals a new beginning and a chance to wipe the old slate clean and start fresh. However, the great thing is that you don't need to wait for the new year to come around to make a big change. A study by Wharton Professor Katherine Milkman showed that people tend to be most motivated on what she calls "temporal landmarks" such as the first day of the week, the start of the new month, the start of new school semesters, birthdays, and other holidays. These fresh start days are a great time to set goals, re-examine your plans, or start something new. Don't wait for New Year's Day to get a fresh start. Instead, make a fresh start as soon as today.

SOURCE: https://pubsonline.informs.org/doi/10.1287/mnsc.2014.1901

WEEKLY BATTLE PLANNING

Week of _____

GOAL REVIEW AND WEEKLY OBJECTIVES

Each week, review your big goals and subsequently break those goals down into objectives, determine the source of your motivation, identify potential roadblocks, and time-block those activities.

GOAL #1 _____

I want this goal because _____

This week, my objective is _____

In pursuit of this objective, the largest roadblock might be _____

...and I'll overcome that roadblock by _____

I will work on this goal on _____
                           (day/time)   (Now, go schedule this on your calendar.)

GOAL #2 _____

I want this goal because _____

This week, my objective is _____

In pursuit of this objective, the largest roadblock might be _____

...and I'll overcome that roadblock by _____

I will work on this goal on _____
                           (day/time)   (Now, go schedule this on your calendar.)

GOAL #3 _____

I want this goal because _____

This week, my objective is _____

In pursuit of this objective, the largest roadblock might be _____

...and I'll overcome that roadblock by _____

I will work on this goal on _____
                           (day/time)   (Now, go schedule this on your calendar.)

The #1 Most Important Thing to move my goals forward this week...	

(Now, go schedule this on your calendar.)

BUILDING AND TRACKING DAILY HABITS

Use the following chart to identify three to six key habits or processes that, when carried out consistently, will result in positive changes and help you achieve your goals. In the first column, identify the habit; in the second, set a goal for the number of times you wish to accomplish this; and then track your progress throughout the week.

Habit/Process	Goal	SUNDAY	MONDAY	TUESDAY	WEDNESDAY	THURSDAY	FRIDAY	SATURDAY	Total

END OF WEEK REVIEW

Looking at your wins and losses from your recent past can help you identify patterns, celebrate wins, determine course corrections, and ultimately lead you closer to your destination.

How did I get closer to my goals this week? _____

_____

What lessons did I learn this week that will help me next week? _____

_____

On a scale of 1–10, with 10 being the highest, I would rate last week's productivity at a _____

Last week I studied...

_____

Next week I'll study...

_____

This week, did I...	Yes	No
take care of my body and mind ?	☐	☐
take care of my relationships?	☐	☐
take enough breaks?	☐	☐
make time for myself?	☐	☐
get enough sleep?	☐	☐

Did I accomplish my #1 most important goal last week? _____

If yes, celebrate! If not, why? _____

MY WEEK _____

MON

TUE

WED

THU

FRI

SAT

SUN

BRAIN DUMP

_____

_____

_____

_____

_____

_____

_____

_____

_____

_____

_____

_____

WEEKLY BATTLE PLANNING

Week of _____

GOAL REVIEW AND WEEKLY OBJECTIVES

Each week, review your big goals and subsequently break those goals down into objectives, determine the source of your motivation, identify potential roadblocks, and time-block those activities.

GOAL #1 _____

I want this goal because _____

This week, my objective is _____

In pursuit of this objective, the largest roadblock might be _____

...and I'll overcome that roadblock by _____

I will work on this goal on _____
(day/time)   (Now, go schedule this on your calendar.)

GOAL #2 _____

I want this goal because _____

This week, my objective is _____

In pursuit of this objective, the largest roadblock might be _____

...and I'll overcome that roadblock by _____

I will work on this goal on _____
(day/time)   (Now, go schedule this on your calendar.)

GOAL #3 _____

I want this goal because _____

This week, my objective is _____

In pursuit of this objective, the largest roadblock might be _____

...and I'll overcome that roadblock by _____

I will work on this goal on _____
(day/time)   (Now, go schedule this on your calendar.)

The #1 Most Important Thing to move my goals forward this week...	

(Now, go schedule this on your calendar.)

BUILDING AND TRACKING DAILY HABITS

Use the following chart to identify three to six key habits or processes that, when carried out consistently, will result in positive changes and help you achieve your goals. In the first column, identify the habit; in the second, set a goal for the number of times you wish to accomplish this; and then track your progress throughout the week.

Habit/Process	Goal	SUNDAY	MONDAY	TUESDAY	WEDNESDAY	THURSDAY	FRIDAY	SATURDAY	Total

END OF WEEK REVIEW

Looking at your wins and losses from your recent past can help you identify patterns, celebrate wins, determine course corrections, and ultimately lead you closer to your destination.

How did I get closer to my goals this week? _____

_____

What lessons did I learn this week that will help me next week? _____

_____

On a scale of 1–10, with 10 being the highest, I would rate last week's productivity at a _____

Last week I studied...

Next week I'll study...

This week, did I...	Yes	No
take care of my body and mind ?	☐	☐
take care of my relationships?	☐	☐
take enough breaks?	☐	☐
make time for myself?	☐	☐
get enough sleep?	☐	☐

Did I accomplish my #1 most important goal last week?		If yes, celebrate! If not, why?	

MY WEEK _____

MON

TUE

WED

THU

FRI

SAT

SUN

BRAIN DUMP

SUCCESS TIP

Change This One Word to Stop Bad Habits

If you're trying to stop a bad habit, such as eating junk food, smoking, or watching too much television, changing one simple word can make a tremendous difference. A study published in *The Journal of Consumer Research* showed that individuals who said "don't" instead of "can't" were almost twice as successful at avoiding negative temptation. Rather than saying, "I can't eat sugar," change your vocabulary to "I don't eat sugar." The emphasis on "don't" helps define your internal identity, where conversely "can't" tells your mind that the restrictions are being placed there by an outside force. So—what "don't" you do anymore?

SOURCE: https://www.jstor.org/stable/10.1086/663212

WEEKLY BATTLE PLANNING

Week of _____

GOAL REVIEW AND WEEKLY OBJECTIVES

Each week, review your big goals and subsequently break those goals down into objectives, determine the source of your motivation, identify potential roadblocks, and time-block those activities.

GOAL #1 _____

I want this goal because _____

This week, my objective is _____

In pursuit of this objective, the largest roadblock might be _____

...and I'll overcome that roadblock by _____

I will work on this goal on _____
(day/time)   (Now, go schedule this on your calendar.)

GOAL #2 _____

I want this goal because _____

This week, my objective is _____

In pursuit of this objective, the largest roadblock might be _____

...and I'll overcome that roadblock by _____

I will work on this goal on _____
(day/time)   (Now, go schedule this on your calendar.)

GOAL #3 _____

I want this goal because _____

This week, my objective is _____

In pursuit of this objective, the largest roadblock might be _____

...and I'll overcome that roadblock by _____

I will work on this goal on _____
(day/time)   (Now, go schedule this on your calendar.)

The #1 Most Important Thing to move my goals forward this week...

(Now, go schedule this on your calendar.)

BUILDING AND TRACKING DAILY HABITS

Use the following chart to identify three to six key habits or processes that, when carried out consistently, will result in positive changes and help you achieve your goals. In the first column, identify the habit; in the second, set a goal for the number of times you wish to accomplish this; and then track your progress throughout the week.

Habit/Process	Goal	SUNDAY	MONDAY	TUESDAY	WEDNESDAY	THURSDAY	FRIDAY	SATURDAY	Total

END OF WEEK REVIEW

Looking at your wins and losses from your recent past can help you identify patterns, celebrate wins, determine course corrections, and ultimately lead you closer to your destination.

How did I get closer to my goals this week? _____

_____

What lessons did I learn this week that will help me next week? _____

_____

On a scale of 1–10, with 10 being the highest, I would rate last week's productivity at a _____

Last week I studied...

Next week I'll study...

This week, did I...	Yes	No
take care of my body and mind ?	☐	☐
take care of my relationships?	☐	☐
take enough breaks?	☐	☐
make time for myself?	☐	☐
get enough sleep?	☐	☐

Did I accomplish my #1 most important goal last week?

If yes, celebrate! If not, why?

MY WEEK _____

MON

TUE

WED

THU

FRI

SAT

SUN

BRAIN DUMP

_____
_____
_____
_____
_____
_____
_____
_____
_____
_____
_____
_____
_____

SUCCESS TIP

A Glutton for Punishment

Everyone loves a reward for accomplishing a task, but research shows that just the opposite might be more effective: punishment for failing to accomplish a task. Researchers at Washington University in St. Louis conducted a study that found punishment may be 200% to 300% more effective than rewards in directing behavior. Of course, a lot depends on the type of reward and punishment being offered, but finding ways to "punish" yourself might be the kick in the pants you need to get your big tasks done. Did you fail to meet your weekly goal? Maybe losing Netflix for a month will be more effective than rewarding yourself with ice cream.

SOURCE: https://source.wustl.edu/2015/05/carrot-or-stick-punishments-may-guide-behavior-more-effectively-than-rewards/

WEEKLY BATTLE PLANNING

Week of _____

GOAL REVIEW AND WEEKLY OBJECTIVES

Each week, review your big goals and subsequently break those goals down into objectives, determine the source of your motivation, identify potential roadblocks, and time-block those activities.

GOAL #1 _____

I want this goal because _____

This week, my objective is _____

In pursuit of this objective, the largest roadblock might be _____

...and I'll overcome that roadblock by _____

I will work on this goal on _____
(day/time)   (Now, go schedule this on your calendar.)

GOAL #2 _____

I want this goal because _____

This week, my objective is _____

In pursuit of this objective, the largest roadblock might be _____

...and I'll overcome that roadblock by _____

I will work on this goal on _____
(day/time)   (Now, go schedule this on your calendar.)

GOAL #3 _____

I want this goal because _____

This week, my objective is _____

In pursuit of this objective, the largest roadblock might be _____

...and I'll overcome that roadblock by _____

I will work on this goal on _____
(day/time)   (Now, go schedule this on your calendar.)

The #1 Most Important Thing to move my goals forward this week...

(Now, go schedule this on your calendar.)

BUILDING AND TRACKING DAILY HABITS

Use the following chart to identify three to six key habits or processes that, when carried out consistently, will result in positive changes and help you achieve your goals. In the first column, identify the habit; in the second, set a goal for the number of times you wish to accomplish this; and then track your progress throughout the week.

Habit/Process	Goal	SUNDAY	MONDAY	TUESDAY	WEDNESDAY	THURSDAY	FRIDAY	SATURDAY	Total

END OF WEEK REVIEW

Looking at your wins and losses from your recent past can help you identify patterns, celebrate wins, determine course corrections, and ultimately lead you closer to your destination.

How did I get closer to my goals this week? _____

_____

What lessons did I learn this week that will help me next week? _____

_____

On a scale of 1–10, with 10 being the highest, I would rate last week's productivity at a _____

Last week I studied...

Next week I'll study...

This week, did I...	Yes	No
take care of my body and mind ?	☐	☐
take care of my relationships?	☐	☐
take enough breaks?	☐	☐
make time for myself?	☐	☐
get enough sleep?	☐	☐

Did I accomplish my #1 most important goal last week?

If yes, celebrate! If not, why?

MY WEEK _____

MON

_____

_____

_____

TUE

_____

_____

_____

_____

WED

_____

_____

_____

_____

THU

_____

_____

_____

_____

FRI

_____

_____

_____

_____

SAT

_____

_____

_____

_____

SUN

_____

_____

_____

BRAIN DUMP

SUCCESS TIP

The Final Piece of the Goal Puzzle

Many have heard that writing down your goals is an effective way to increase the odds of the goal being reached—and a study by Gail Matthews of Dominican University backs up that belief, showing an almost 40% increase in goal completion for those who write down their goals. But adding another piece to the goal puzzle increased the completion rate even higher: weekly accountability. The participants in the study who wrote their goals down and received a weekly accountability check-in from a friend saw a 77% increase in the probability that their goal would be reached. So, how can you add in some accountability into your life? Join a Mastermind group on BiggerPockets.com/start!

SOURCE: https://www.dominican.edu/academics/lae/undergraduate-programs/psych/faculty/assets-gail-matthews/researchsummary2.pdf

WEEKLY BATTLE PLANNING

Week of _____

GOAL REVIEW AND WEEKLY OBJECTIVES

Each week, review your big goals and subsequently break those goals down into objectives, determine the source of your motivation, identify potential roadblocks, and time-block those activities.

GOAL #1 _____

I want this goal because _____

This week, my objective is _____

In pursuit of this objective, the largest roadblock might be _____

...and I'll overcome that roadblock by _____

I will work on this goal on _____
                            (day/time)   (Now, go schedule this on your calendar.)

GOAL #2 _____

I want this goal because _____

This week, my objective is _____

In pursuit of this objective, the largest roadblock might be _____

...and I'll overcome that roadblock by _____

I will work on this goal on _____
                            (day/time)   (Now, go schedule this on your calendar.)

GOAL #3 _____

I want this goal because _____

This week, my objective is _____

In pursuit of this objective, the largest roadblock might be _____

...and I'll overcome that roadblock by _____

I will work on this goal on _____
                            (day/time)   (Now, go schedule this on your calendar.)

The #1 Most Important Thing to move my goals forward this week...	

(Now, go schedule this on your calendar.)

BUILDING AND TRACKING DAILY HABITS

Use the following chart to identify three to six key habits or processes that, when carried out consistently, will result in positive changes and help you achieve your goals. In the first column, identify the habit; in the second, set a goal for the number of times you wish to accomplish this; and then track your progress throughout the week.

Habit/Process	Goal	SUNDAY	MONDAY	TUESDAY	WEDNESDAY	THURSDAY	FRIDAY	SATURDAY	Total

END OF WEEK REVIEW

Looking at your wins and losses from your recent past can help you identify patterns, celebrate wins, determine course corrections, and ultimately lead you closer to your destination.

How did I get closer to my goals this week? _____

_____

What lessons did I learn this week that will help me next week? _____

_____

On a scale of 1–10, with 10 being the highest, I would rate last week's productivity at a _____

Last week I studied...

Next week I'll study...

This week, did I...	Yes	No
take care of my body and mind ?	☐	☐
take care of my relationships?	☐	☐
take enough breaks?	☐	☐
make time for myself?	☐	☐
get enough sleep?	☐	☐

Did I accomplish my #1 most important goal last week?

If yes, celebrate! If not, why?

MY WEEK _____

MON

TUE

WED

THU

FRI

SAT

SUN

BRAIN DUMP

WEEKLY BATTLE PLANNING

Week of _____

GOAL REVIEW AND WEEKLY OBJECTIVES

Each week, review your big goals and subsequently break those goals down into objectives, determine the source of your motivation, identify potential roadblocks, and time-block those activities.

GOAL #1 _____

I want this goal because _____

This week, my objective is _____

In pursuit of this objective, the largest roadblock might be _____

...and I'll overcome that roadblock by _____

I will work on this goal on _____
                          (day/time)   (Now, go schedule this on your calendar.)

GOAL #2 _____

I want this goal because _____

This week, my objective is _____

In pursuit of this objective, the largest roadblock might be _____

...and I'll overcome that roadblock by _____

I will work on this goal on _____
                          (day/time)   (Now, go schedule this on your calendar.)

GOAL #3 _____

I want this goal because _____

This week, my objective is _____

In pursuit of this objective, the largest roadblock might be _____

...and I'll overcome that roadblock by _____

I will work on this goal on _____
                          (day/time)   (Now, go schedule this on your calendar.)

The #1 Most Important Thing to move my goals forward this week...	

(Now, go schedule this on your calendar.)

BUILDING AND TRACKING DAILY HABITS

Use the following chart to identify three to six key habits or processes that, when carried out consistently, will result in positive changes and help you achieve your goals. In the first column, identify the habit; in the second, set a goal for the number of times you wish to accomplish this; and then track your progress throughout the week.

Habit/Process	Goal	SUNDAY	MONDAY	TUESDAY	WEDNESDAY	THURSDAY	FRIDAY	SATURDAY	Total

END OF WEEK REVIEW

Looking at your wins and losses from your recent past can help you identify patterns, celebrate wins, determine course corrections, and ultimately lead you closer to your destination.

How did I get closer to my goals this week? _____

_____

What lessons did I learn this week that will help me next week? _____

_____

On a scale of 1–10, with 10 being the highest, I would rate last week's productivity at a _____

Last week I studied...
Next week I'll study...

This week, did I...	Yes	No
take care of my body and mind ?	☐	☐
take care of my relationships?	☐	☐
take enough breaks?	☐	☐
make time for myself?	☐	☐
get enough sleep?	☐	☐

Did I accomplish my #1 most important goal last week?		If yes, celebrate! If not, why?	

MY WEEK _____

MON

TUE

WED

THU

FRI

SAT

SUN

BRAIN DUMP

WEEKLY BATTLE PLANNING

Week of _____ _____

GOAL REVIEW AND WEEKLY OBJECTIVES

Each week, review your big goals and subsequently break those goals down into objectives, determine the source of your motivation, identify potential roadblocks, and time-block those activities.

GOAL #1 _____

I want this goal because _____

This week, my objective is _____

In pursuit of this objective, the largest roadblock might be _____

...and I'll overcome that roadblock by _____

I will work on this goal on _____
              (day/time)   (Now, go schedule this on your calendar.)

GOAL #2 _____

I want this goal because _____

This week, my objective is _____

In pursuit of this objective, the largest roadblock might be _____

...and I'll overcome that roadblock by _____

I will work on this goal on _____
              (day/time)   (Now, go schedule this on your calendar.)

GOAL #3 _____

I want this goal because _____

This week, my objective is _____

In pursuit of this objective, the largest roadblock might be _____

...and I'll overcome that roadblock by _____

I will work on this goal on _____
              (day/time)   (Now, go schedule this on your calendar.)

The #1 Most Important Thing to move my goals forward this week...

(Now, go schedule this on your calendar.)

BUILDING AND TRACKING DAILY HABITS

Use the following chart to identify three to six key habits or processes that, when carried out consistently, will result in positive changes and help you achieve your goals. In the first column, identify the habit; in the second, set a goal for the number of times you wish to accomplish this; and then track your progress throughout the week.

Habit/Process	Goal	SUNDAY	MONDAY	TUESDAY	WEDNESDAY	THURSDAY	FRIDAY	SATURDAY	Total

END OF WEEK REVIEW

Looking at your wins and losses from your recent past can help you identify patterns, celebrate wins, determine course corrections, and ultimately lead you closer to your destination.

How did I get closer to my goals this week? _____

_____

What lessons did I learn this week that will help me next week? _____

_____

On a scale of 1–10, with 10 being the highest, I would rate last week's productivity at a _____

Last week I studied...	This week, did I...	Yes	No
	take care of my body and mind ?	☐	☐
Next week I'll study...	take care of my relationships?	☐	☐
	take enough breaks?	☐	☐
	make time for myself?	☐	☐
	get enough sleep?	☐	☐

Did I accomplish my #1 most important goal last week?		If yes, celebrate! If not, why?	

MY WEEK _____

MON

_____
_____
_____
_____

TUE

_____
_____
_____
_____

WED

_____
_____
_____
_____

THU

_____
_____
_____
_____

FRI

_____
_____
_____
_____

SAT

_____
_____
_____
_____

SUN

_____
_____
_____
_____

BRAIN DUMP

WEEKLY BATTLE PLANNING

Week of _____ _____

GOAL REVIEW AND WEEKLY OBJECTIVES

Each week, review your big goals and subsequently break those goals down into objectives, determine the source of your motivation, identify potential roadblocks, and time-block those activities.

GOAL #1 _____

I want this goal because _____

This week, my objective is _____

In pursuit of this objective, the largest roadblock might be _____

...and I'll overcome that roadblock by _____

I will work on this goal on _____
　　　　　　　　　　　　　　　(day/time)　　　　　　　(Now, go schedule this on your calendar.)

GOAL #2 _____

I want this goal because _____

This week, my objective is _____

In pursuit of this objective, the largest roadblock might be _____

...and I'll overcome that roadblock by _____

I will work on this goal on _____
　　　　　　　　　　　　　　　(day/time)　　　　　　　(Now, go schedule this on your calendar.)

GOAL #3 _____

I want this goal because _____

This week, my objective is _____

In pursuit of this objective, the largest roadblock might be _____

...and I'll overcome that roadblock by _____

I will work on this goal on _____
　　　　　　　　　　　　　　　(day/time)　　　　　　　(Now, go schedule this on your calendar.)

The #1 Most Important Thing to move my goals forward this week...	

(Now, go schedule this on your calendar.)

BUILDING AND TRACKING DAILY HABITS

Use the following chart to identify three to six key habits or processes that, when carried out consistently, will result in positive changes and help you achieve your goals. In the first column, identify the habit; in the second, set a goal for the number of times you wish to accomplish this; and then track your progress throughout the week.

Habit/Process	Goal	SUNDAY	MONDAY	TUESDAY	WEDNESDAY	THURSDAY	FRIDAY	SATURDAY	Total

END OF WEEK REVIEW

Looking at your wins and losses from your recent past can help you identify patterns, celebrate wins, determine course corrections, and ultimately lead you closer to your destination.

How did I get closer to my goals this week? _____

_____

What lessons did I learn this week that will help me next week? _____

_____

On a scale of 1–10, with 10 being the highest, I would rate last week's productivity at a _____

Last week I studied...

Next week I'll study...

This week, did I...	Yes	No
take care of my body and mind ?	☐	☐
take care of my relationships?	☐	☐
take enough breaks?	☐	☐
make time for myself?	☐	☐
get enough sleep?	☐	☐

Did I accomplish my #1 most important goal last week?

If yes, celebrate! If not, why?

MY WEEK _____

MON

_____
_____
_____
_____

TUE

_____
_____
_____
_____

WED

_____
_____
_____
_____

THU

_____
_____
_____
_____

FRI

_____
_____
_____
_____

SAT

_____
_____
_____
_____

SUN

_____
_____
_____
_____

BRAIN DUMP

WEEKLY BATTLE PLANNING

Week of _____

GOAL REVIEW AND WEEKLY OBJECTIVES

Each week, review your big goals and subsequently break those goals down into objectives, determine the source of your motivation, identify potential roadblocks, and time-block those activities.

GOAL #1 _____

I want this goal because _____

This week, my objective is _____

In pursuit of this objective, the largest roadblock might be _____

...and I'll overcome that roadblock by _____

I will work on this goal on _____

(day/time)   (Now, go schedule this on your calendar.)

GOAL #2 _____

I want this goal because _____

This week, my objective is _____

In pursuit of this objective, the largest roadblock might be _____

...and I'll overcome that roadblock by _____

I will work on this goal on _____

(day/time)   (Now, go schedule this on your calendar.)

GOAL #3 _____

I want this goal because _____

This week, my objective is _____

In pursuit of this objective, the largest roadblock might be _____

...and I'll overcome that roadblock by _____

I will work on this goal on _____

(day/time)   (Now, go schedule this on your calendar.)

The #1 Most Important Thing to move my goals forward this week...

(Now, go schedule this on your calendar.)

BUILDING AND TRACKING DAILY HABITS

Use the following chart to identify three to six key habits or processes that, when carried out consistently, will result in positive changes and help you achieve your goals. In the first column, identify the habit; in the second, set a goal for the number of times you wish to accomplish this; and then track your progress throughout the week.

Habit/Process	Goal	SUNDAY	MONDAY	TUESDAY	WEDNESDAY	THURSDAY	FRIDAY	SATURDAY	Total

END OF WEEK REVIEW

Looking at your wins and losses from your recent past can help you identify patterns, celebrate wins, determine course corrections, and ultimately lead you closer to your destination.

How did I get closer to my goals this week? _____

_____

What lessons did I learn this week that will help me next week? _____

_____

On a scale of 1–10, with 10 being the highest, I would rate last week's productivity at a _____

Last week I studied...
Next week I'll study...

This week, did I...	Yes	No
take care of my body and mind ?	☐	☐
take care of my relationships?	☐	☐
take enough breaks?	☐	☐
make time for myself?	☐	☐
get enough sleep?	☐	☐

Did I accomplish my #1 most important goal last week?		If yes, celebrate! If not, why?	

MY WEEK _____

MON

TUE

WED

THU

FRI

SAT

SUN

BRAIN DUMP

WEEKLY BATTLE PLANNING

Week of _____

GOAL REVIEW AND WEEKLY OBJECTIVES

Each week, review your big goals and subsequently break those goals down into objectives, determine the source of your motivation, identify potential roadblocks, and time-block those activities.

GOAL #1 _____

I want this goal because _____

This week, my objective is _____

In pursuit of this objective, the largest roadblock might be _____

...and I'll overcome that roadblock by _____

I will work on this goal on _____
(day/time) (Now, go schedule this on your calendar.)

GOAL #2 _____

I want this goal because _____

This week, my objective is _____

In pursuit of this objective, the largest roadblock might be _____

...and I'll overcome that roadblock by _____

I will work on this goal on _____
(day/time) (Now, go schedule this on your calendar.)

GOAL #3 _____

I want this goal because _____

This week, my objective is _____

In pursuit of this objective, the largest roadblock might be _____

...and I'll overcome that roadblock by _____

I will work on this goal on _____
(day/time) (Now, go schedule this on your calendar.)

The #1 Most Important Thing to move my goals forward this week...	

(Now, go schedule this on your calendar.)

BUILDING AND TRACKING DAILY HABITS

Use the following chart to identify three to six key habits or processes that, when carried out consistently, will result in positive changes and help you achieve your goals. In the first column, identify the habit; in the second, set a goal for the number of times you wish to accomplish this; and then track your progress throughout the week.

Habit/Process	Goal	SUNDAY	MONDAY	TUESDAY	WEDNESDAY	THURSDAY	FRIDAY	SATURDAY	Total

END OF WEEK REVIEW

Looking at your wins and losses from your recent past can help you identify patterns, celebrate wins, determine course corrections, and ultimately lead you closer to your destination.

How did I get closer to my goals this week? _____

_____

What lessons did I learn this week that will help me next week? _____

_____

On a scale of 1–10, with 10 being the highest, I would rate last week's productivity at a _____

Last week I studied...	This week, did I...	Yes	No
	take care of my body and mind ?	☐	☐
Next week I'll study...	take care of my relationships?	☐	☐
	take enough breaks?	☐	☐
	make time for myself?	☐	☐
	get enough sleep?	☐	☐

Did I accomplish my #1 most important goal last week?		If yes, celebrate! If not, why?	

MY WEEK _____

MON

TUE

WED

THU

FRI

SAT

SUN

BRAIN DUMP

_____

_____

_____

_____

_____

_____

_____

_____

_____

_____

_____

_____

WEEKLY BATTLE PLANNING

Week of _____

GOAL REVIEW AND WEEKLY OBJECTIVES

Each week, review your big goals and subsequently break those goals down into objectives, determine the source of your motivation, identify potential roadblocks, and time-block those activities.

GOAL #1 _____

I want this goal because _____

This week, my objective is _____

In pursuit of this objective, the largest roadblock might be _____

...and I'll overcome that roadblock by _____

I will work on this goal on _____
(day/time)   (Now, go schedule this on your calendar.)

GOAL #2 _____

I want this goal because _____

This week, my objective is _____

In pursuit of this objective, the largest roadblock might be _____

...and I'll overcome that roadblock by _____

I will work on this goal on _____
(day/time)   (Now, go schedule this on your calendar.)

GOAL #3 _____

I want this goal because _____

This week, my objective is _____

In pursuit of this objective, the largest roadblock might be _____

...and I'll overcome that roadblock by _____

I will work on this goal on _____
(day/time)   (Now, go schedule this on your calendar.)

The #1 Most Important Thing to move my goals forward this week...	

(Now, go schedule this on your calendar.)

BUILDING AND TRACKING DAILY HABITS

Use the following chart to identify three to six key habits or processes that, when carried out consistently, will result in positive changes and help you achieve your goals. In the first column, identify the habit; in the second, set a goal for the number of times you wish to accomplish this; and then track your progress throughout the week.

Habit/Process	Goal	SUNDAY	MONDAY	TUESDAY	WEDNESDAY	THURSDAY	FRIDAY	SATURDAY	Total

END OF WEEK REVIEW

Looking at your wins and losses from your recent past can help you identify patterns, celebrate wins, determine course corrections, and ultimately lead you closer to your destination.

How did I get closer to my goals this week? _____

_____

What lessons did I learn this week that will help me next week? _____

_____

On a scale of 1–10, with 10 being the highest, I would rate last week's productivity at a _____

Last week I studied...

Next week I'll study...

This week, did I...	Yes	No
take care of my body and mind ?	☐	☐
take care of my relationships?	☐	☐
take enough breaks?	☐	☐
make time for myself?	☐	☐
get enough sleep?	☐	☐

Did I accomplish my #1 most important goal last week?

If yes, celebrate! If not, why?

MY WEEK _____

MON

TUE

WED

THU

FRI

SAT

SUN

BRAIN DUMP

_____

_____

_____

_____

_____

_____

_____

_____

_____

_____

_____

SUCCESS TIP

A Better Smile to Make People Like and Trust You!

Many areas of life are improved when others simply like you; and one of the best ways to get someone to like you, according to research by Stanford University, is to smile. However, not all smiles are the same. According to a paper published in _The Pacific Northwest Journal of Undergraduate Research and Creative Activities_, the most trust and positive emotions about a person are elicited by a Duchenne smile! A Duchenne is a smile where the eyes are wrinkled or squinted along with the upturn of the mouth, as opposed to a "Pan Am" smile which involves only the mouth. Try it right now—which smile feels more genuine?

SOURCE: https://journals.plos.org/plosone/article?id=10.1371/journal.pone.0161794
SOURCE: https://commons.pacificu.edu/pnwestjurca/vol2/iss1/3/

WEEKLY BATTLE PLANNING

Week of _____

GOAL REVIEW AND WEEKLY OBJECTIVES

Each week, review your big goals and subsequently break those goals down into objectives, determine the source of your motivation, identify potential roadblocks, and time-block those activities.

GOAL #1 _____

I want this goal because _____

This week, my objective is _____

In pursuit of this objective, the largest roadblock might be _____

...and I'll overcome that roadblock by _____

I will work on this goal on _____

(day/time)   (Now, go schedule this on your calendar.)

GOAL #2 _____

I want this goal because _____

This week, my objective is _____

In pursuit of this objective, the largest roadblock might be _____

...and I'll overcome that roadblock by _____

I will work on this goal on _____

(day/time)   (Now, go schedule this on your calendar.)

GOAL #3 _____

I want this goal because _____

This week, my objective is _____

In pursuit of this objective, the largest roadblock might be _____

...and I'll overcome that roadblock by _____

I will work on this goal on _____

(day/time)   (Now, go schedule this on your calendar.)

The #1 Most Important Thing to move my goals forward this week...	

(Now, go schedule this on your calendar.)

BUILDING AND TRACKING DAILY HABITS

Use the following chart to identify three to six key habits or processes that, when carried out consistently, will result in positive changes and help you achieve your goals. In the first column, identify the habit; in the second, set a goal for the number of times you wish to accomplish this; and then track your progress throughout the week.

Habit/Process	Goal	SUNDAY	MONDAY	TUESDAY	WEDNESDAY	THURSDAY	FRIDAY	SATURDAY	Total

END OF WEEK REVIEW

Looking at your wins and losses from your recent past can help you identify patterns, celebrate wins, determine course corrections, and ultimately lead you closer to your destination.

How did I get closer to my goals this week? _____

_____

What lessons did I learn this week that will help me next week? _____

_____

On a scale of 1–10, with 10 being the highest, I would rate last week's productivity at a _____

Last week I studied...

Next week I'll study...

This week, did I...	Yes	No
take care of my body and mind ?	☐	☐
take care of my relationships?	☐	☐
take enough breaks?	☐	☐
make time for myself?	☐	☐
get enough sleep?	☐	☐

Did I accomplish my #1 most important goal last week?

If yes, celebrate! If not, why?

MY WEEK _____

MON

TUE

WED

THU

FRI

SAT

SUN

BRAIN DUMP

DAILY ACTION PLANS

DAILY ACTION PLAN
MORNING ROUTINE

Hours Slept _____   Wake-up Time _____

Water ☐   Daily Journal ☐   _____ ☐   _____ ☐

This morning, I'm grateful for _____

GOALS AND M.I.N.S.

Goals are important to review daily, reinforcing your objectives to your conscious and subconscious mind. But goals alone are not enough. It's also vital that you take time to identify your Most Important Next Step (M.I.N.S.) for each goal, so your goal transforms into an action. And remember, when it comes to M.I.N.S., be specific.

GOAL #1 _____

Weekly Objective: _____

M.I.N.S. _____

GOAL #2 _____

Weekly Objective: _____

M.I.N.S. _____

GOAL #3 _____

Weekly Objective: _____

M.I.N.S. _____

I can consider today a "win" if I...

This is your #1 Most Important Thing!

TODAY'S TIME-BLOCKING ACTIVITIES

High-achievers know that what gets scheduled gets done. Take a few minutes to think about your goals, your M.I.N.S., and schedule your day. Don't forget to include several breaks.

5:00 _____	11:00 _____	5:00 _____
5:30 _____	11:30 _____	5:30 _____
6:00 _____	12:00 _____	6:00 _____
6:30 _____	12:30 _____	6:30 _____
7:00 _____	1:00 _____	7:00 _____
7:30 _____	1:30 _____	7:30 _____
8:00 _____	2:00 _____	8:00 _____
8:30 _____	2:30 _____	8:30 _____
9:00 _____	3:00 _____	9:00 _____
9:30 _____	3:30 _____	9:30 _____
10:00 _____	4:00 _____	10:00 _____
10:30 _____	4:30 _____	10:30 _____

☐ Did I include enough breaks in the day?

☐ Did I schedule my #1 Most Important Thing?

EVENING REVIEW

Did you accomplish your #1 Most Important Thing today? Yes ☐ No ☐

Today was awesome because _____

_____

Today I struggled with _____

_____

On a scale of 1–10, with 10 being the highest, I would rate today's productivity at a _____

Tomorrow I will...   Notes

_____   _____

_____   _____

_____   _____

DAILY ACTION PLAN
MORNING ROUTINE

Hours Slept _____ Wake-up Time _____

Water ☐ Daily Journal ☐ _____ ☐ _____ ☐

This morning, I'm grateful for _____

GOALS AND M.I.N.S.

Goals are important to review daily, reinforcing your objectives to your conscious and subconscious mind. But goals alone are not enough. It's also vital that you take time to identify your Most Important Next Step (M.I.N.S.) for each goal, so your goal transforms into an action. And remember, when it comes to M.I.N.S., be specific.

GOAL #1 _____

Weekly Objective: _____

M.I.N.S. _____

GOAL #2 _____

Weekly Objective: _____

M.I.N.S. _____

GOAL #3 _____

Weekly Objective: _____

M.I.N.S. _____

I can consider today a "win" if I...

This is your #1 Most Important Thing!

TODAY'S TIME-BLOCKING ACTIVITIES

High-achievers know that what gets scheduled gets done. Take a few minutes to think about your goals, your M.I.N.S., and schedule your day. Don't forget to include several breaks.

5:00 _____	11:00 _____	5:00 _____
5:30 _____	11:30 _____	5:30 _____
6:00 _____	12:00 _____	6:00 _____
6:30 _____	12:30 _____	6:30 _____
7:00 _____	1:00 _____	7:00 _____
7:30 _____	1:30 _____	7:30 _____
8:00 _____	2:00 _____	8:00 _____
8:30 _____	2:30 _____	8:30 _____
9:00 _____	3:00 _____	9:00 _____
9:30 _____	3:30 _____	9:30 _____
10:00 _____	4:00 _____	10:00 _____
10:30 _____	4:30 _____	10:30 _____

☐ Did I include enough breaks in the day?

☐ Did I schedule my #1 Most Important Thing?

EVENING REVIEW

Did you accomplish your #1 Most Important Thing today?   Yes ☐   No ☐

Today was awesome because _____

_____

Today I struggled with _____

_____

On a scale of 1–10, with 10 being the highest, I would rate today's productivity at a _____

Tomorrow I will...   Notes

_____   _____

_____   _____

_____   _____

DAILY ACTION PLAN
MORNING ROUTINE

Hours Slept _____ Wake-up Time _____

Water ☐ Daily Journal ☐ _____ ☐ _____ ☐

This morning, I'm grateful for _____

GOALS AND M.I.N.S.

Goals are important to review daily, reinforcing your objectives to your conscious and subconscious mind. But goals alone are not enough. It's also vital that you take time to identify your Most Important Next Step (M.I.N.S.) for each goal, so your goal transforms into an action. And remember, when it comes to M.I.N.S., be specific.

GOAL #1 _____

Weekly Objective: _____

M.I.N.S. _____

GOAL #2 _____

Weekly Objective: _____

M.I.N.S. _____

GOAL #3 _____

Weekly Objective: _____

M.I.N.S. _____

I can consider today a "win" if I...

This is your #1 Most Important Thing!

TODAY'S TIME-BLOCKING ACTIVITIES

High-achievers know that what gets scheduled gets done. Take a few minutes to think about your goals, your M.I.N.S., and schedule your day. Don't forget to include several breaks.

5:00 _____	11:00 _____	5:00 _____
5:30 _____	11:30 _____	5:30 _____
6:00 _____	12:00 _____	6:00 _____
6:30 _____	12:30 _____	6:30 _____
7:00 _____	1:00 _____	7:00 _____
7:30 _____	1:30 _____	7:30 _____
8:00 _____	2:00 _____	8:00 _____
8:30 _____	2:30 _____	8:30 _____
9:00 _____	3:00 _____	9:00 _____
9:30 _____	3:30 _____	9:30 _____
10:00 _____	4:00 _____	10:00 _____
10:30 _____	4:30 _____	10:30 _____

☐ Did I include enough breaks in the day?

☐ Did I schedule my #1 Most Important Thing?

EVENING REVIEW

Did you accomplish your #1 Most Important Thing today?   Yes ☐   No ☐

Today was awesome because _____

_____

Today I struggled with _____

_____

On a scale of 1–10, with 10 being the highest, I would rate today's productivity at a _____

Tomorrow I will...   Notes

_____   _____

_____   _____

_____   _____

DAILY ACTION PLAN

MORNING ROUTINE

Hours Slept _____   Wake-up Time _____

Water ☐   Daily Journal ☐   _____ ☐   _____ ☐

This morning, I'm grateful for _____

GOALS AND M.I.N.S.

Goals are important to review daily, reinforcing your objectives to your conscious and subconscious mind. But goals alone are not enough. It's also vital that you take time to identify your Most Important Next Step (M.I.N.S.) for each goal, so your goal transforms into an action. And remember, when it comes to M.I.N.S., be specific.

GOAL #1 _____

Weekly Objective: _____

M.I.N.S. _____

GOAL #2 _____

Weekly Objective: _____

M.I.N.S. _____

GOAL #3 _____

Weekly Objective: _____

M.I.N.S. _____

I can consider today a "win" if I...

This is your #1 Most Important Thing!

TODAY'S TIME-BLOCKING ACTIVITIES

High-achievers know that what gets scheduled gets done. Take a few minutes to think about your goals, your M.I.N.S., and schedule your day. Don't forget to include several breaks.

5:00 _____	11:00 _____	5:00 _____
5:30 _____	11:30 _____	5:30 _____
6:00 _____	12:00 _____	6:00 _____
6:30 _____	12:30 _____	6:30 _____
7:00 _____	1:00 _____	7:00 _____
7:30 _____	1:30 _____	7:30 _____
8:00 _____	2:00 _____	8:00 _____
8:30 _____	2:30 _____	8:30 _____
9:00 _____	3:00 _____	9:00 _____
9:30 _____	3:30 _____	9:30 _____
10:00 _____	4:00 _____	10:00 _____
10:30 _____	4:30 _____	10:30 _____

☐ Did I include enough breaks in the day?

☐ Did I schedule my #1 Most Important Thing?

EVENING REVIEW

Did you accomplish your #1 Most Important Thing today?   Yes ☐   No ☐

Today was awesome because _____

_____

Today I struggled with _____

_____

On a scale of 1–10, with 10 being the highest, I would rate today's productivity at a _____

Tomorrow I will...   Notes

_____   _____

_____   _____

_____   _____

DAILY ACTION PLAN
MORNING ROUTINE

Hours Slept _____   Wake-up Time _____

Water ☐   Daily Journal ☐   _____ ☐   _____ ☐

This morning, I'm grateful for _____

GOALS AND M.I.N.S.

Goals are important to review daily, reinforcing your objectives to your conscious and subconscious mind. But goals alone are not enough. It's also vital that you take time to identify your Most Important Next Step (M.I.N.S.) for each goal, so your goal transforms into an action. And remember, when it comes to M.I.N.S., be specific.

GOAL #1 _____

Weekly Objective: _____

M.I.N.S. _____

GOAL #2 _____

Weekly Objective: _____

M.I.N.S. _____

GOAL #3 _____

Weekly Objective: _____

M.I.N.S. _____

I can consider today a "win" if I...

This is your #1 Most Important Thing!

TODAY'S TIME-BLOCKING ACTIVITIES

High-achievers know that what gets scheduled gets done. Take a few minutes to think about your goals, your M.I.N.S., and schedule your day. Don't forget to include several breaks.

5:00 _____	11:00 _____	5:00 _____
5:30 _____	11:30 _____	5:30 _____
6:00 _____	12:00 _____	6:00 _____
6:30 _____	12:30 _____	6:30 _____
7:00 _____	1:00 _____	7:00 _____
7:30 _____	1:30 _____	7:30 _____
8:00 _____	2:00 _____	8:00 _____
8:30 _____	2:30 _____	8:30 _____
9:00 _____	3:00 _____	9:00 _____
9:30 _____	3:30 _____	9:30 _____
10:00 _____	4:00 _____	10:00 _____
10:30 _____	4:30 _____	10:30 _____

☐ Did I include enough breaks in the day?   ☐ Did I schedule my #1 Most Important Thing?

EVENING REVIEW

Did you accomplish your #1 Most Important Thing today?   Yes ☐   No ☐

Today was awesome because _____

_____

Today I struggled with _____

_____

On a scale of 1–10, with 10 being the highest, I would rate today's productivity at a _____

Tomorrow I will...   Notes

_____   _____

_____   _____

_____   _____

DAILY ACTION PLAN

MORNING ROUTINE

Hours Slept _____   Wake-up Time _____

Water ☐   Daily Journal ☐   _____ ☐   _____ ☐

This morning, I'm grateful for _____

GOALS AND M.I.N.S.

Goals are important to review daily, reinforcing your objectives to your conscious and subconscious mind. But goals alone are not enough. It's also vital that you take time to identify your Most Important Next Step (M.I.N.S.) for each goal, so your goal transforms into an action. And remember, when it comes to M.I.N.S., be specific.

GOAL #1 _____

Weekly Objective: _____

M.I.N.S. _____

GOAL #2 _____

Weekly Objective: _____

M.I.N.S. _____

GOAL #3 _____

Weekly Objective: _____

M.I.N.S. _____

I can consider today a "win" if I...

This is your #1 Most Important Thing!

TODAY'S TIME-BLOCKING ACTIVITIES

High-achievers know that what gets scheduled gets done. Take a few minutes to think about your goals, your M.I.N.S., and schedule your day. Don't forget to include several breaks.

5:00 _____	11:00 _____	5:00 _____
5:30 _____	11:30 _____	5:30 _____
6:00 _____	12:00 _____	6:00 _____
6:30 _____	12:30 _____	6:30 _____
7:00 _____	1:00 _____	7:00 _____
7:30 _____	1:30 _____	7:30 _____
8:00 _____	2:00 _____	8:00 _____
8:30 _____	2:30 _____	8:30 _____
9:00 _____	3:00 _____	9:00 _____
9:30 _____	3:30 _____	9:30 _____
10:00 _____	4:00 _____	10:00 _____
10:30 _____	4:30 _____	10:30 _____

☐ Did I include enough breaks in the day?　　☐ Did I schedule my #1 Most Important Thing?

EVENING REVIEW

Did you accomplish your #1 Most Important Thing today?　Yes ☐　No ☐

Today was awesome because _____

_____

Today I struggled with _____

_____

On a scale of 1–10, with 10 being the highest, I would rate today's productivity at a _____

Tomorrow I will...　　　　　　　　　　　Notes

_____　　　　_____

_____　　　　_____

_____　　　　_____

DAILY ACTION PLAN

MORNING ROUTINE

Hours Slept _____ Wake-up Time _____

Water ☐ Daily Journal ☐   _____ ☐   _____ ☐

This morning, I'm grateful for _____

GOALS AND M.I.N.S.

Goals are important to review daily, reinforcing your objectives to your conscious and subconscious mind. But goals alone are not enough. It's also vital that you take time to identify your Most Important Next Step (M.I.N.S.) for each goal, so your goal transforms into an action. And remember, when it comes to M.I.N.S., be specific.

GOAL #1 _____

Weekly Objective: _____

M.I.N.S. _____

GOAL #2 _____

Weekly Objective: _____

M.I.N.S. _____

GOAL #3 _____

Weekly Objective: _____

M.I.N.S. _____

I can consider today a "win" if I...

This is your #1 Most Important Thing!

TODAY'S TIME-BLOCKING ACTIVITIES

High-achievers know that what gets scheduled gets done. Take a few minutes to think about your goals, your M.I.N.S., and schedule your day. Don't forget to include several breaks.

5:00 _____	11:00 _____	5:00 _____
5:30 _____	11:30 _____	5:30 _____
6:00 _____	12:00 _____	6:00 _____
6:30 _____	12:30 _____	6:30 _____
7:00 _____	1:00 _____	7:00 _____
7:30 _____	1:30 _____	7:30 _____
8:00 _____	2:00 _____	8:00 _____
8:30 _____	2:30 _____	8:30 _____
9:00 _____	3:00 _____	9:00 _____
9:30 _____	3:30 _____	9:30 _____
10:00 _____	4:00 _____	10:00 _____
10:30 _____	4:30 _____	10:30 _____

☐ Did I include enough breaks in the day?

☐ Did I schedule my #1 Most Important Thing?

EVENING REVIEW

Did you accomplish your #1 Most Important Thing today?   Yes ☐   No ☐

Today was awesome because _____

_____

Today I struggled with _____

_____

On a scale of 1–10, with 10 being the highest, I would rate today's productivity at a _____

Tomorrow I will...   Notes

_____   _____

_____   _____

_____   _____

DAILY ACTION PLAN

MORNING ROUTINE

Hours Slept _____ Wake-up Time _____

Water ☐ Daily Journal ☐ _____ ☐ _____ ☐

This morning, I'm grateful for _____

GOALS AND M.I.N.S.

Goals are important to review daily, reinforcing your objectives to your conscious and subconscious mind. But goals alone are not enough. It's also vital that you take time to identify your Most Important Next Step (M.I.N.S.) for each goal, so your goal transforms into an action. And remember, when it comes to M.I.N.S., be specific.

GOAL #1 _____

Weekly Objective: _____

M.I.N.S. _____

GOAL #2 _____

Weekly Objective: _____

M.I.N.S. _____

GOAL #3 _____

Weekly Objective: _____

M.I.N.S. _____

I can consider today a "win" if I...

This is your #1 Most Important Thing!

TODAY'S TIME-BLOCKING ACTIVITIES

High-achievers know that what gets scheduled gets done. Take a few minutes to think about your goals, your M.I.N.S., and schedule your day. Don't forget to include several breaks.

5:00 _____	11:00 _____	5:00 _____
5:30 _____	11:30 _____	5:30 _____
6:00 _____	12:00 _____	6:00 _____
6:30 _____	12:30 _____	6:30 _____
7:00 _____	1:00 _____	7:00 _____
7:30 _____	1:30 _____	7:30 _____
8:00 _____	2:00 _____	8:00 _____
8:30 _____	2:30 _____	8:30 _____
9:00 _____	3:00 _____	9:00 _____
9:30 _____	3:30 _____	9:30 _____
10:00 _____	4:00 _____	10:00 _____
10:30 _____	4:30 _____	10:30 _____

☐ Did I include enough breaks in the day?

☐ Did I schedule my #1 Most Important Thing?

EVENING REVIEW

Did you accomplish your #1 Most Important Thing today?   Yes ☐   No ☐

Today was awesome because _____

_____

Today I struggled with _____

_____

On a scale of 1–10, with 10 being the highest, I would rate today's productivity at a _____

Tomorrow I will...   Notes

_____   _____

_____   _____

_____   _____

DAILY ACTION PLAN

MORNING ROUTINE

Hours Slept _____   Wake-up Time _____

Water ☐   Daily Journal ☐   _____ ☐   _____ ☐

This morning, I'm grateful for _____

GOALS AND M.I.N.S.

Goals are important to review daily, reinforcing your objectives to your conscious and subconscious mind. But goals alone are not enough. It's also vital that you take time to identify your Most Important Next Step (M.I.N.S.) for each goal, so your goal transforms into an action. And remember, when it comes to M.I.N.S., be specific.

GOAL #1 _____

Weekly Objective: _____

M.I.N.S. _____

GOAL #2 _____

Weekly Objective: _____

M.I.N.S. _____

GOAL #3 _____

Weekly Objective: _____

M.I.N.S. _____

I can consider today a "win" if I...

This is your #1 Most Important Thing!

TODAY'S TIME-BLOCKING ACTIVITIES

High-achievers know that what gets scheduled gets done. Take a few minutes to think about your goals, your M.I.N.S., and schedule your day. Don't forget to include several breaks.

5:00 _____	11:00 _____	5:00 _____
5:30 _____	11:30 _____	5:30 _____
6:00 _____	12:00 _____	6:00 _____
6:30 _____	12:30 _____	6:30 _____
7:00 _____	1:00 _____	7:00 _____
7:30 _____	1:30 _____	7:30 _____
8:00 _____	2:00 _____	8:00 _____
8:30 _____	2:30 _____	8:30 _____
9:00 _____	3:00 _____	9:00 _____
9:30 _____	3:30 _____	9:30 _____
10:00 _____	4:00 _____	10:00 _____
10:30 _____	4:30 _____	10:30 _____

☐ Did I include enough breaks in the day?

☐ Did I schedule my #1 Most Important Thing?

EVENING REVIEW

Did you accomplish your #1 Most Important Thing today?   Yes ☐   No ☐

Today was awesome because _____

_____

Today I struggled with _____

_____

On a scale of 1–10, with 10 being the highest, I would rate today's productivity at a _____

Tomorrow I will...   Notes

_____   _____

_____   _____

_____   _____

DAILY ACTION PLAN
MORNING ROUTINE

Hours Slept _____   Wake-up Time _____

Water ☐   Daily Journal ☐   _____ ☐   _____ ☐

This morning, I'm grateful for _____

GOALS AND M.I.N.S.

Goals are important to review daily, reinforcing your objectives to your conscious and subconscious mind. But goals alone are not enough. It's also vital that you take time to identify your Most Important Next Step (M.I.N.S.) for each goal, so your goal transforms into an action. And remember, when it comes to M.I.N.S., be specific.

GOAL #1 _____

Weekly Objective: _____

M.I.N.S. _____

GOAL #2 _____

Weekly Objective: _____

M.I.N.S. _____

GOAL #3 _____

Weekly Objective: _____

M.I.N.S. _____

I can consider today a "win" if I...

This is your #1 Most Important Thing!

TODAY'S TIME-BLOCKING ACTIVITIES

High-achievers know that what gets scheduled gets done. Take a few minutes to think about your goals, your M.I.N.S., and schedule your day. Don't forget to include several breaks.

5:00 _____	11:00 _____	5:00 _____
5:30 _____	11:30 _____	5:30 _____
6:00 _____	12:00 _____	6:00 _____
6:30 _____	12:30 _____	6:30 _____
7:00 _____	1:00 _____	7:00 _____
7:30 _____	1:30 _____	7:30 _____
8:00 _____	2:00 _____	8:00 _____
8:30 _____	2:30 _____	8:30 _____
9:00 _____	3:00 _____	9:00 _____
9:30 _____	3:30 _____	9:30 _____
10:00 _____	4:00 _____	10:00 _____
10:30 _____	4:30 _____	10:30 _____

☐ Did I include enough breaks in the day?

☐ Did I schedule my #1 Most Important Thing?

EVENING REVIEW

Did you accomplish your #1 Most Important Thing today?   Yes ☐   No ☐

Today was awesome because _____

_____

Today I struggled with _____

_____

On a scale of 1–10, with 10 being the highest, I would rate today's productivity at a _____

Tomorrow I will...   Notes

_____   _____

_____   _____

_____   _____

DAILY ACTION PLAN
MORNING ROUTINE

Hours Slept _____   Wake-up Time _____

Water ☐   Daily Journal ☐   _____ ☐   _____ ☐

This morning, I'm grateful for _____

GOALS AND M.I.N.S.

Goals are important to review daily, reinforcing your objectives to your conscious and subconscious mind. But goals alone are not enough. It's also vital that you take time to identify your Most Important Next Step (M.I.N.S.) for each goal, so your goal transforms into an action. And remember, when it comes to M.I.N.S., be specific.

GOAL #1 _____

Weekly Objective: _____

M.I.N.S. _____

GOAL #2 _____

Weekly Objective: _____

M.I.N.S. _____

GOAL #3 _____

Weekly Objective: _____

M.I.N.S. _____

I can consider today a "win" if I...

This is your #1 Most Important Thing!

TODAY'S TIME-BLOCKING ACTIVITIES

High-achievers know that what gets scheduled gets done. Take a few minutes to think about your goals, your M.I.N.S., and schedule your day. Don't forget to include several breaks.

5:00	11:00	5:00
5:30	11:30	5:30
6:00	12:00	6:00
6:30	12:30	6:30
7:00	1:00	7:00
7:30	1:30	7:30
8:00	2:00	8:00
8:30	2:30	8:30
9:00	3:00	9:00
9:30	3:30	9:30
10:00	4:00	10:00
10:30	4:30	10:30

☐ Did I include enough breaks in the day?

☐ Did I schedule my #1 Most Important Thing?

EVENING REVIEW

Did you accomplish your #1 Most Important Thing today?   Yes ☐   No ☐

Today was awesome because _____

_____

Today I struggled with _____

_____

On a scale of 1–10, with 10 being the highest, I would rate today's productivity at a _____

Tomorrow I will...

Notes

DAILY ACTION PLAN
MORNING ROUTINE

Hours Slept _____   Wake-up Time _____

Water ☐   Daily Journal ☐   _____ ☐   _____ ☐

This morning, I'm grateful for _____

GOALS AND M.I.N.S.

Goals are important to review daily, reinforcing your objectives to your conscious and subconscious mind. But goals alone are not enough. It's also vital that you take time to identify your Most Important Next Step (M.I.N.S.) for each goal, so your goal transforms into an action. And remember, when it comes to M.I.N.S., be specific.

GOAL #1 _____

Weekly Objective: _____

M.I.N.S. _____

GOAL #2 _____

Weekly Objective: _____

M.I.N.S. _____

GOAL #3 _____

Weekly Objective: _____

M.I.N.S. _____

I can consider today a "win" if I...

This is your #1 Most Important Thing!

TODAY'S TIME-BLOCKING ACTIVITIES

High-achievers know that what gets scheduled gets done. Take a few minutes to think about your goals, your M.I.N.S., and schedule your day. Don't forget to include several breaks.

5:00 _____	11:00 _____	5:00 _____
5:30 _____	11:30 _____	5:30 _____
6:00 _____	12:00 _____	6:00 _____
6:30 _____	12:30 _____	6:30 _____
7:00 _____	1:00 _____	7:00 _____
7:30 _____	1:30 _____	7:30 _____
8:00 _____	2:00 _____	8:00 _____
8:30 _____	2:30 _____	8:30 _____
9:00 _____	3:00 _____	9:00 _____
9:30 _____	3:30 _____	9:30 _____
10:00 _____	4:00 _____	10:00 _____
10:30 _____	4:30 _____	10:30 _____

☐ Did I include enough breaks in the day?   ☐ Did I schedule my #1 Most Important Thing?

EVENING REVIEW

Did you accomplish your #1 Most Important Thing today?   Yes ☐   No ☐

Today was awesome because _____

_____

Today I struggled with _____

_____

On a scale of 1–10, with 10 being the highest, I would rate today's productivity at a _____

Tomorrow I will...   Notes

_____   _____

_____   _____

_____   _____

DAILY ACTION PLAN
MORNING ROUTINE

Hours Slept _____   Wake-up Time _____

Water ☐   Daily Journal ☐   _____ ☐   _____ ☐

This morning, I'm grateful for _____

GOALS AND M.I.N.S.

Goals are important to review daily, reinforcing your objectives to your conscious and subconscious mind. But goals alone are not enough. It's also vital that you take time to identify your Most Important Next Step (M.I.N.S.) for each goal, so your goal transforms into an action. And remember, when it comes to M.I.N.S., be specific.

GOAL #1 _____

Weekly Objective: _____

M.I.N.S. _____

GOAL #2 _____

Weekly Objective: _____

M.I.N.S. _____

GOAL #3 _____

Weekly Objective: _____

M.I.N.S. _____

I can consider today a "win" if I...

This is your #1 Most Important Thing!

TODAY'S TIME-BLOCKING ACTIVITIES

High-achievers know that what gets scheduled gets done. Take a few minutes to think about your goals, your M.I.N.S., and schedule your day. Don't forget to include several breaks.

5:00 _____	11:00 _____	5:00 _____
5:30 _____	11:30 _____	5:30 _____
6:00 _____	12:00 _____	6:00 _____
6:30 _____	12:30 _____	6:30 _____
7:00 _____	1:00 _____	7:00 _____
7:30 _____	1:30 _____	7:30 _____
8:00 _____	2:00 _____	8:00 _____
8:30 _____	2:30 _____	8:30 _____
9:00 _____	3:00 _____	9:00 _____
9:30 _____	3:30 _____	9:30 _____
10:00 _____	4:00 _____	10:00 _____
10:30 _____	4:30 _____	10:30 _____

☐ Did I include enough breaks in the day?

☐ Did I schedule my #1 Most Important Thing?

EVENING REVIEW

Did you accomplish your #1 Most Important Thing today?　Yes ☐　No ☐

Today was awesome because _____

_____

Today I struggled with _____

_____

On a scale of 1–10, with 10 being the highest, I would rate today's productivity at a _____

Tomorrow I will...

Notes

_____　_____

_____　_____

_____　_____

DAILY ACTION PLAN
MORNING ROUTINE

Hours Slept _____ Wake-up Time _____

Water ☐ Daily Journal ☐ _____ ☐ _____ ☐

This morning, I'm grateful for _____

GOALS AND M.I.N.S.

Goals are important to review daily, reinforcing your objectives to your conscious and subconscious mind. But goals alone are not enough. It's also vital that you take time to identify your Most Important Next Step (M.I.N.S.) for each goal, so your goal transforms into an action. And remember, when it comes to M.I.N.S., be specific.

GOAL #1 _____

Weekly Objective: _____

M.I.N.S. _____

GOAL #2 _____

Weekly Objective: _____

M.I.N.S. _____

GOAL #3 _____

Weekly Objective: _____

M.I.N.S. _____

I can consider today a "win" if I...

This is your #1 Most Important Thing!

TODAY'S TIME-BLOCKING ACTIVITIES

High-achievers know that what gets scheduled gets done. Take a few minutes to think about your goals, your M.I.N.S., and schedule your day. Don't forget to include several breaks.

5:00 _____	11:00 _____	5:00 _____
5:30 _____	11:30 _____	5:30 _____
6:00 _____	12:00 _____	6:00 _____
6:30 _____	12:30 _____	6:30 _____
7:00 _____	1:00 _____	7:00 _____
7:30 _____	1:30 _____	7:30 _____
8:00 _____	2:00 _____	8:00 _____
8:30 _____	2:30 _____	8:30 _____
9:00 _____	3:00 _____	9:00 _____
9:30 _____	3:30 _____	9:30 _____
10:00 _____	4:00 _____	10:00 _____
10:30 _____	4:30 _____	10:30 _____

☐ Did I include enough breaks in the day?　　☐ Did I schedule my #1 Most Important Thing?

EVENING REVIEW

Did you accomplish your #1 Most Important Thing today?　Yes ☐　No ☐

Today was awesome because _____

_____

Today I struggled with _____

_____

On a scale of 1–10, with 10 being the highest, I would rate today's productivity at a _____

Tomorrow I will...　　　　　　　　　　Notes

_____　　　　_____

_____　　　　_____

_____　　　　_____

DAILY ACTION PLAN
MORNING ROUTINE

Hours Slept _____ Wake-up Time _____

Water ☐ Daily Journal ☐ _____ ☐ _____ ☐

This morning, I'm grateful for _____

GOALS AND M.I.N.S.

Goals are important to review daily, reinforcing your objectives to your conscious and subconscious mind. But goals alone are not enough. It's also vital that you take time to identify your Most Important Next Step (M.I.N.S.) for each goal, so your goal transforms into an action. And remember, when it comes to M.I.N.S., be specific.

GOAL #1 _____

Weekly Objective: _____

M.I.N.S. _____

GOAL #2 _____

Weekly Objective: _____

M.I.N.S. _____

GOAL #3 _____

Weekly Objective: _____

M.I.N.S. _____

I can consider today a "win" if I...

This is your #1 Most Important Thing!

TODAY'S TIME-BLOCKING ACTIVITIES

High-achievers know that what gets scheduled gets done. Take a few minutes to think about your goals, your M.I.N.S., and schedule your day. Don't forget to include several breaks.

5:00 _____	11:00 _____	5:00 _____
5:30 _____	11:30 _____	5:30 _____
6:00 _____	12:00 _____	6:00 _____
6:30 _____	12:30 _____	6:30 _____
7:00 _____	1:00 _____	7:00 _____
7:30 _____	1:30 _____	7:30 _____
8:00 _____	2:00 _____	8:00 _____
8:30 _____	2:30 _____	8:30 _____
9:00 _____	3:00 _____	9:00 _____
9:30 _____	3:30 _____	9:30 _____
10:00 _____	4:00 _____	10:00 _____
10:30 _____	4:30 _____	10:30 _____

☐ Did I include enough breaks in the day?

☐ Did I schedule my #1 Most Important Thing?

EVENING REVIEW

Did you accomplish your #1 Most Important Thing today?   Yes ☐   No ☐

Today was awesome because _____

_____

Today I struggled with _____

_____

On a scale of 1–10, with 10 being the highest, I would rate today's productivity at a _____

Tomorrow I will...   Notes

_____   _____

_____   _____

_____   _____

DAILY ACTION PLAN

MORNING ROUTINE

Hours Slept _____   Wake-up Time _____

Water ☐   Daily Journal ☐   _____ ☐   _____ ☐

This morning, I'm grateful for _____

GOALS AND M.I.N.S.

Goals are important to review daily, reinforcing your objectives to your conscious and subconscious mind. But goals alone are not enough. It's also vital that you take time to identify your Most Important Next Step (M.I.N.S.) for each goal, so your goal transforms into an action. And remember, when it comes to M.I.N.S., be specific.

GOAL #1 _____

Weekly Objective: _____

M.I.N.S. _____

GOAL #2 _____

Weekly Objective: _____

M.I.N.S. _____

GOAL #3 _____

Weekly Objective: _____

M.I.N.S. _____

I can consider today a "win" if I...

This is your #1 Most Important Thing!

TODAY'S TIME-BLOCKING ACTIVITIES

High-achievers know that what gets scheduled gets done. Take a few minutes to think about your goals, your M.I.N.S., and schedule your day. Don't forget to include several breaks.

5:00 _____	11:00 _____	5:00 _____
5:30 _____	11:30 _____	5:30 _____
6:00 _____	12:00 _____	6:00 _____
6:30 _____	12:30 _____	6:30 _____
7:00 _____	1:00 _____	7:00 _____
7:30 _____	1:30 _____	7:30 _____
8:00 _____	2:00 _____	8:00 _____
8:30 _____	2:30 _____	8:30 _____
9:00 _____	3:00 _____	9:00 _____
9:30 _____	3:30 _____	9:30 _____
10:00 _____	4:00 _____	10:00 _____
10:30 _____	4:30 _____	10:30 _____

☐ Did I include enough breaks in the day? ☐ Did I schedule my #1 Most Important Thing?

EVENING REVIEW

Did you accomplish your #1 Most Important Thing today? Yes ☐ No ☐

Today was awesome because _____

_____

Today I struggled with _____

_____

On a scale of 1–10, with 10 being the highest, I would rate today's productivity at a _____

Tomorrow I will...   Notes

_____   _____

_____   _____

_____   _____

DAILY ACTION PLAN

MORNING ROUTINE

Hours Slept _____ Wake-up Time _____

Water ☐ Daily Journal ☐ _____ ☐ _____ ☐

This morning, I'm grateful for _____

GOALS AND M.I.N.S.

Goals are important to review daily, reinforcing your objectives to your conscious and subconscious mind. But goals alone are not enough. It's also vital that you take time to identify your Most Important Next Step (M.I.N.S.) for each goal, so your goal transforms into an action. And remember, when it comes to M.I.N.S., be specific.

GOAL #1 _____

Weekly Objective: _____

M.I.N.S. _____

GOAL #2 _____

Weekly Objective: _____

M.I.N.S. _____

GOAL #3 _____

Weekly Objective: _____

M.I.N.S. _____

I can consider today a "win" if I...

This is your #1 Most Important Thing!

TODAY'S TIME-BLOCKING ACTIVITIES

High-achievers know that what gets scheduled gets done. Take a few minutes to think about your goals, your M.I.N.S., and schedule your day. Don't forget to include several breaks.

5:00 _____	11:00 _____	5:00 _____
5:30 _____	11:30 _____	5:30 _____
6:00 _____	12:00 _____	6:00 _____
6:30 _____	12:30 _____	6:30 _____
7:00 _____	1:00 _____	7:00 _____
7:30 _____	1:30 _____	7:30 _____
8:00 _____	2:00 _____	8:00 _____
8:30 _____	2:30 _____	8:30 _____
9:00 _____	3:00 _____	9:00 _____
9:30 _____	3:30 _____	9:30 _____
10:00 _____	4:00 _____	10:00 _____
10:30 _____	4:30 _____	10:30 _____

☐ Did I include enough breaks in the day?

☐ Did I schedule my #1 Most Important Thing?

EVENING REVIEW

Did you accomplish your #1 Most Important Thing today? Yes ☐ No ☐

Today was awesome because _____

_____

Today I struggled with _____

_____

On a scale of 1–10, with 10 being the highest, I would rate today's productivity at a _____

Tomorrow I will...

Notes

_____ _____

_____ _____

_____ _____

DAILY ACTION PLAN
MORNING ROUTINE

Hours Slept _____ Wake-up Time _____

Water ☐ Daily Journal ☐ _____ ☐ _____ ☐

This morning, I'm grateful for _____

GOALS AND M.I.N.S.

Goals are important to review daily, reinforcing your objectives to your conscious and subconscious mind. But goals alone are not enough. It's also vital that you take time to identify your Most Important Next Step (M.I.N.S.) for each goal, so your goal transforms into an action. And remember, when it comes to M.I.N.S., be specific.

GOAL #1 _____

Weekly Objective: _____

M.I.N.S. _____

GOAL #2 _____

Weekly Objective: _____

M.I.N.S. _____

GOAL #3 _____

Weekly Objective: _____

M.I.N.S. _____

I can consider today a "win" if I...

This is your #1 Most Important Thing!

TODAY'S TIME-BLOCKING ACTIVITIES

High-achievers know that what gets scheduled gets done. Take a few minutes to think about your goals, your M.I.N.S., and schedule your day. Don't forget to include several breaks.

5:00 _____	11:00 _____	5:00 _____
5:30 _____	11:30 _____	5:30 _____
6:00 _____	12:00 _____	6:00 _____
6:30 _____	12:30 _____	6:30 _____
7:00 _____	1:00 _____	7:00 _____
7:30 _____	1:30 _____	7:30 _____
8:00 _____	2:00 _____	8:00 _____
8:30 _____	2:30 _____	8:30 _____
9:00 _____	3:00 _____	9:00 _____
9:30 _____	3:30 _____	9:30 _____
10:00 _____	4:00 _____	10:00 _____
10:30 _____	4:30 _____	10:30 _____

☐ Did I include enough breaks in the day?   ☐ Did I schedule my #1 Most Important Thing?

EVENING REVIEW

Did you accomplish your #1 Most Important Thing today?   Yes ☐   No ☐

Today was awesome because _____

_____

Today I struggled with _____

_____

On a scale of 1–10, with 10 being the highest, I would rate today's productivity at a _____

Tomorrow I will...   Notes

_____   _____

_____   _____

_____   _____

DAILY ACTION PLAN
MORNING ROUTINE

Hours Slept _____ Wake-up Time _____

Water ☐   Daily Journal ☐   _____ ☐   _____ ☐

This morning, I'm grateful for _____

GOALS AND M.I.N.S.

Goals are important to review daily, reinforcing your objectives to your conscious and subconscious mind. But goals alone are not enough. It's also vital that you take time to identify your Most Important Next Step (M.I.N.S.) for each goal, so your goal transforms into an action. And remember, when it comes to M.I.N.S., be specific.

GOAL #1 _____

Weekly Objective: _____

M.I.N.S. _____

GOAL #2 _____

Weekly Objective: _____

M.I.N.S. _____

GOAL #3 _____

Weekly Objective: _____

M.I.N.S. _____

I can consider today a "win" if I...

This is your #1 Most Important Thing!

TODAY'S TIME-BLOCKING ACTIVITIES

High-achievers know that what gets scheduled gets done. Take a few minutes to think about your goals, your M.I.N.S., and schedule your day. Don't forget to include several breaks.

5:00 _____	11:00 _____	5:00 _____
5:30 _____	11:30 _____	5:30 _____
6:00 _____	12:00 _____	6:00 _____
6:30 _____	12:30 _____	6:30 _____
7:00 _____	1:00 _____	7:00 _____
7:30 _____	1:30 _____	7:30 _____
8:00 _____	2:00 _____	8:00 _____
8:30 _____	2:30 _____	8:30 _____
9:00 _____	3:00 _____	9:00 _____
9:30 _____	3:30 _____	9:30 _____
10:00 _____	4:00 _____	10:00 _____
10:30 _____	4:30 _____	10:30 _____

☐ Did I include enough breaks in the day?

☐ Did I schedule my #1 Most Important Thing?

EVENING REVIEW

Did you accomplish your #1 Most Important Thing today?   Yes ☐   No ☐

Today was awesome because _____

_____

Today I struggled with _____

_____

On a scale of 1–10, with 10 being the highest, I would rate today's productivity at a _____

Tomorrow I will...

Notes

_____   _____

_____   _____

_____   _____

DAILY ACTION PLAN

MORNING ROUTINE

Hours Slept _____ Wake-up Time _____

Water ☐ Daily Journal ☐ _____ ☐ _____ ☐

This morning, I'm grateful for _____

GOALS AND M.I.N.S.

Goals are important to review daily, reinforcing your objectives to your conscious and subconscious mind. But goals alone are not enough. It's also vital that you take time to identify your Most Important Next Step (M.I.N.S.) for each goal, so your goal transforms into an action. And remember, when it comes to M.I.N.S., be specific.

GOAL #1 _____

Weekly Objective: _____

M.I.N.S. _____

GOAL #2 _____

Weekly Objective: _____

M.I.N.S. _____

GOAL #3 _____

Weekly Objective: _____

M.I.N.S. _____

I can consider today a "win" if I...

This is your #1 Most Important Thing!

TODAY'S TIME-BLOCKING ACTIVITIES

High-achievers know that what gets scheduled gets done. Take a few minutes to think about your goals, your M.I.N.S., and schedule your day. Don't forget to include several breaks.

5:00 _____	11:00 _____	5:00 _____
5:30 _____	11:30 _____	5:30 _____
6:00 _____	12:00 _____	6:00 _____
6:30 _____	12:30 _____	6:30 _____
7:00 _____	1:00 _____	7:00 _____
7:30 _____	1:30 _____	7:30 _____
8:00 _____	2:00 _____	8:00 _____
8:30 _____	2:30 _____	8:30 _____
9:00 _____	3:00 _____	9:00 _____
9:30 _____	3:30 _____	9:30 _____
10:00 _____	4:00 _____	10:00 _____
10:30 _____	4:30 _____	10:30 _____

☐ Did I include enough breaks in the day?

☐ Did I schedule my #1 Most Important Thing?

EVENING REVIEW

Did you accomplish your #1 Most Important Thing today?   Yes ☐   No ☐

Today was awesome because _____

_____

Today I struggled with _____

_____

On a scale of 1–10, with 10 being the highest, I would rate today's productivity at a _____

Tomorrow I will...   Notes

_____   _____

_____   _____

_____   _____

DAILY ACTION PLAN
MORNING ROUTINE

Hours Slept _____   Wake-up Time _____

Water ☐   Daily Journal ☐   _____ ☐   _____ ☐

This morning, I'm grateful for _____

GOALS AND M.I.N.S.

Goals are important to review daily, reinforcing your objectives to your conscious and subconscious mind. But goals alone are not enough. It's also vital that you take time to identify your Most Important Next Step (M.I.N.S.) for each goal, so your goal transforms into an action. And remember, when it comes to M.I.N.S., be specific.

GOAL #1 _____

Weekly Objective: _____

M.I.N.S. _____

GOAL #2 _____

Weekly Objective: _____

M.I.N.S. _____

GOAL #3 _____

Weekly Objective: _____

M.I.N.S. _____

I can consider today a "win" if I...

This is your #1 Most Important Thing!

TODAY'S TIME-BLOCKING ACTIVITIES

High-achievers know that what gets scheduled gets done. Take a few minutes to think about your goals, your M.I.N.S., and schedule your day. Don't forget to include several breaks.

5:00 _____	11:00 _____	5:00 _____
5:30 _____	11:30 _____	5:30 _____
6:00 _____	12:00 _____	6:00 _____
6:30 _____	12:30 _____	6:30 _____
7:00 _____	1:00 _____	7:00 _____
7:30 _____	1:30 _____	7:30 _____
8:00 _____	2:00 _____	8:00 _____
8:30 _____	2:30 _____	8:30 _____
9:00 _____	3:00 _____	9:00 _____
9:30 _____	3:30 _____	9:30 _____
10:00 _____	4:00 _____	10:00 _____
10:30 _____	4:30 _____	10:30 _____

☐ Did I include enough breaks in the day?

☐ Did I schedule my #1 Most Important Thing?

EVENING REVIEW

Did you accomplish your #1 Most Important Thing today?   Yes ☐   No ☐

Today was awesome because _____

_____

Today I struggled with _____

_____

On a scale of 1–10, with 10 being the highest, I would rate today's productivity at a _____

Tomorrow I will...   Notes

_____   _____

_____   _____

_____   _____

DAILY ACTION PLAN
MORNING ROUTINE

Hours Slept _____   Wake-up Time _____

Water ☐   Daily Journal ☐   _____ ☐   _____ ☐

This morning, I'm grateful for _____

GOALS AND M.I.N.S.

Goals are important to review daily, reinforcing your objectives to your conscious and subconscious mind. But goals alone are not enough. It's also vital that you take time to identify your Most Important Next Step (M.I.N.S.) for each goal, so your goal transforms into an action. And remember, when it comes to M.I.N.S., be specific.

GOAL #1 _____

Weekly Objective: _____

M.I.N.S. _____

GOAL #2 _____

Weekly Objective: _____

M.I.N.S. _____

GOAL #3 _____

Weekly Objective: _____

M.I.N.S. _____

I can consider today a "win" if I...

This is your #1 Most Important Thing!

TODAY'S TIME-BLOCKING ACTIVITIES

High-achievers know that what gets scheduled gets done. Take a few minutes to think about your goals, your M.I.N.S., and schedule your day. Don't forget to include several breaks.

5:00 _____	11:00 _____	5:00 _____
5:30 _____	11:30 _____	5:30 _____
6:00 _____	12:00 _____	6:00 _____
6:30 _____	12:30 _____	6:30 _____
7:00 _____	1:00 _____	7:00 _____
7:30 _____	1:30 _____	7:30 _____
8:00 _____	2:00 _____	8:00 _____
8:30 _____	2:30 _____	8:30 _____
9:00 _____	3:00 _____	9:00 _____
9:30 _____	3:30 _____	9:30 _____
10:00 _____	4:00 _____	10:00 _____
10:30 _____	4:30 _____	10:30 _____

☐ Did I include enough breaks in the day?

☐ Did I schedule my #1 Most Important Thing?

EVENING REVIEW

Did you accomplish your #1 Most Important Thing today?   Yes ☐   No ☐

Today was awesome because _____

_____

Today I struggled with _____

_____

On a scale of 1–10, with 10 being the highest, I would rate today's productivity at a _____

Tomorrow I will...   Notes

_____   _____

_____   _____

_____   _____

DAILY ACTION PLAN
MORNING ROUTINE

Hours Slept _____ Wake-up Time _____

Water ☐   Daily Journal ☐   _____ ☐   _____ ☐

This morning, I'm grateful for _____

GOALS AND M.I.N.S.

Goals are important to review daily, reinforcing your objectives to your conscious and subconscious mind. But goals alone are not enough. It's also vital that you take time to identify your Most Important Next Step (M.I.N.S.) for each goal, so your goal transforms into an action. And remember, when it comes to M.I.N.S., be specific.

GOAL #1 _____

Weekly Objective: _____

M.I.N.S. _____

GOAL #2 _____

Weekly Objective: _____

M.I.N.S. _____

GOAL #3 _____

Weekly Objective: _____

M.I.N.S. _____

I can consider today a "win" if I...

This is your #1 Most Important Thing!

TODAY'S TIME-BLOCKING ACTIVITIES

High-achievers know that what gets scheduled gets done. Take a few minutes to think about your goals, your M.I.N.S., and schedule your day. Don't forget to include several breaks.

5:00 _____	11:00 _____	5:00 _____
5:30 _____	11:30 _____	5:30 _____
6:00 _____	12:00 _____	6:00 _____
6:30 _____	12:30 _____	6:30 _____
7:00 _____	1:00 _____	7:00 _____
7:30 _____	1:30 _____	7:30 _____
8:00 _____	2:00 _____	8:00 _____
8:30 _____	2:30 _____	8:30 _____
9:00 _____	3:00 _____	9:00 _____
9:30 _____	3:30 _____	9:30 _____
10:00 _____	4:00 _____	10:00 _____
10:30 _____	4:30 _____	10:30 _____

☐ Did I include enough breaks in the day?

☐ Did I schedule my #1 Most Important Thing?

EVENING REVIEW

Did you accomplish your #1 Most Important Thing today? Yes ☐ No ☐

Today was awesome because _____

_____

Today I struggled with _____

_____

On a scale of 1–10, with 10 being the highest, I would rate today's productivity at a _____

Tomorrow I will...

_____

_____

_____

Notes

_____

_____

_____

DAILY ACTION PLAN
MORNING ROUTINE

Hours Slept _____   Wake-up Time _____

Water ☐   Daily Journal ☐   _____ ☐   _____ ☐

This morning, I'm grateful for _____

GOALS AND M.I.N.S.

Goals are important to review daily, reinforcing your objectives to your conscious and subconscious mind. But goals alone are not enough. It's also vital that you take time to identify your Most Important Next Step (M.I.N.S.) for each goal, so your goal transforms into an action. And remember, when it comes to M.I.N.S., be specific.

GOAL #1 _____

Weekly Objective: _____

M.I.N.S. _____

GOAL #2 _____

Weekly Objective: _____

M.I.N.S. _____

GOAL #3 _____

Weekly Objective: _____

M.I.N.S. _____

I can consider today a "win" if I...

This is your #1 Most Important Thing!

TODAY'S TIME-BLOCKING ACTIVITIES

High-achievers know that what gets scheduled gets done. Take a few minutes to think about your goals, your M.I.N.S., and schedule your day. Don't forget to include several breaks.

5:00 _____	11:00 _____	5:00 _____
5:30 _____	11:30 _____	5:30 _____
6:00 _____	12:00 _____	6:00 _____
6:30 _____	12:30 _____	6:30 _____
7:00 _____	1:00 _____	7:00 _____
7:30 _____	1:30 _____	7:30 _____
8:00 _____	2:00 _____	8:00 _____
8:30 _____	2:30 _____	8:30 _____
9:00 _____	3:00 _____	9:00 _____
9:30 _____	3:30 _____	9:30 _____
10:00 _____	4:00 _____	10:00 _____
10:30 _____	4:30 _____	10:30 _____

☐ Did I include enough breaks in the day?

☐ Did I schedule my #1 Most Important Thing?

EVENING REVIEW

Did you accomplish your #1 Most Important Thing today?   Yes ☐   No ☐

Today was awesome because _____

_____

Today I struggled with _____

_____

On a scale of 1–10, with 10 being the highest, I would rate today's productivity at a _____

Tomorrow I will...

Notes

_____   _____

_____   _____

_____   _____

DAILY ACTION PLAN
MORNING ROUTINE

Hours Slept _____   Wake-up Time _____

Water ☐   Daily Journal ☐   _____ ☐   _____ ☐

This morning, I'm grateful for _____

GOALS AND M.I.N.S.

Goals are important to review daily, reinforcing your objectives to your conscious and subconscious mind. But goals alone are not enough. It's also vital that you take time to identify your Most Important Next Step (M.I.N.S.) for each goal, so your goal transforms into an action. And remember, when it comes to M.I.N.S., be specific.

GOAL #1 _____

Weekly Objective: _____

M.I.N.S. _____

GOAL #2 _____

Weekly Objective: _____

M.I.N.S. _____

GOAL #3 _____

Weekly Objective: _____

M.I.N.S. _____

I can consider today a "win" if I...

This is your #1 Most Important Thing!

TODAY'S TIME-BLOCKING ACTIVITIES

High-achievers know that what gets scheduled gets done. Take a few minutes to think about your goals, your M.I.N.S., and schedule your day. Don't forget to include several breaks.

5:00 _____	11:00 _____	5:00 _____
5:30 _____	11:30 _____	5:30 _____
6:00 _____	12:00 _____	6:00 _____
6:30 _____	12:30 _____	6:30 _____
7:00 _____	1:00 _____	7:00 _____
7:30 _____	1:30 _____	7:30 _____
8:00 _____	2:00 _____	8:00 _____
8:30 _____	2:30 _____	8:30 _____
9:00 _____	3:00 _____	9:00 _____
9:30 _____	3:30 _____	9:30 _____
10:00 _____	4:00 _____	10:00 _____
10:30 _____	4:30 _____	10:30 _____

☐ Did I include enough breaks in the day?

☐ Did I schedule my #1 Most Important Thing?

EVENING REVIEW

Did you accomplish your #1 Most Important Thing today?   Yes ☐   No ☐

Today was awesome because _____

_____

Today I struggled with _____

_____

On a scale of 1–10, with 10 being the highest, I would rate today's productivity at a _____

Tomorrow I will...   Notes

_____   _____

_____   _____

_____   _____

DAILY ACTION PLAN
MORNING ROUTINE

Hours Slept _____ Wake-up Time _____

Water ☐ Daily Journal ☐ _____ ☐ _____ ☐

This morning, I'm grateful for _____

GOALS AND M.I.N.S.

Goals are important to review daily, reinforcing your objectives to your conscious and subconscious mind. But goals alone are not enough. It's also vital that you take time to identify your Most Important Next Step (M.I.N.S.) for each goal, so your goal transforms into an action. And remember, when it comes to M.I.N.S., be specific.

GOAL #1 _____

Weekly Objective: _____

M.I.N.S. _____

GOAL #2 _____

Weekly Objective: _____

M.I.N.S. _____

GOAL #3 _____

Weekly Objective: _____

M.I.N.S. _____

I can consider today a "win" if I...

This is your #1 Most Important Thing!

TODAY'S TIME-BLOCKING ACTIVITIES

High-achievers know that what gets scheduled gets done. Take a few minutes to think about your goals, your M.I.N.S., and schedule your day. Don't forget to include several breaks.

5:00 _____	11:00 _____	5:00 _____
5:30 _____	11:30 _____	5:30 _____
6:00 _____	12:00 _____	6:00 _____
6:30 _____	12:30 _____	6:30 _____
7:00 _____	1:00 _____	7:00 _____
7:30 _____	1:30 _____	7:30 _____
8:00 _____	2:00 _____	8:00 _____
8:30 _____	2:30 _____	8:30 _____
9:00 _____	3:00 _____	9:00 _____
9:30 _____	3:30 _____	9:30 _____
10:00 _____	4:00 _____	10:00 _____
10:30 _____	4:30 _____	10:30 _____

☐ Did I include enough breaks in the day?

☐ Did I schedule my #1 Most Important Thing?

EVENING REVIEW

Did you accomplish your #1 Most Important Thing today?   Yes ☐   No ☐

Today was awesome because _____

_____

Today I struggled with _____

_____

On a scale of 1–10, with 10 being the highest, I would rate today's productivity at a _____

Tomorrow I will...   Notes

_____   _____

_____   _____

_____   _____

DAILY ACTION PLAN
MORNING ROUTINE

Hours Slept _____   Wake-up Time _____

Water ☐   Daily Journal ☐   _____ ☐   _____ ☐

This morning, I'm grateful for _____

GOALS AND M.I.N.S.

Goals are important to review daily, reinforcing your objectives to your conscious and subconscious mind. But goals alone are not enough. It's also vital that you take time to identify your Most Important Next Step (M.I.N.S.) for each goal, so your goal transforms into an action. And remember, when it comes to M.I.N.S., be specific.

GOAL #1 _____

Weekly Objective: _____

M.I.N.S. _____

GOAL #2 _____

Weekly Objective: _____

M.I.N.S. _____

GOAL #3 _____

Weekly Objective: _____

M.I.N.S. _____

I can consider today a "win" if I...

This is your #1 Most Important Thing!

TODAY'S TIME-BLOCKING ACTIVITIES

High-achievers know that what gets scheduled gets done. Take a few minutes to think about your goals, your M.I.N.S., and schedule your day. Don't forget to include several breaks.

5:00 _____	11:00 _____	5:00 _____
5:30 _____	11:30 _____	5:30 _____
6:00 _____	12:00 _____	6:00 _____
6:30 _____	12:30 _____	6:30 _____
7:00 _____	1:00 _____	7:00 _____
7:30 _____	1:30 _____	7:30 _____
8:00 _____	2:00 _____	8:00 _____
8:30 _____	2:30 _____	8:30 _____
9:00 _____	3:00 _____	9:00 _____
9:30 _____	3:30 _____	9:30 _____
10:00 _____	4:00 _____	10:00 _____
10:30 _____	4:30 _____	10:30 _____

☐ Did I include enough breaks in the day?

☐ Did I schedule my #1 Most Important Thing?

EVENING REVIEW

Did you accomplish your #1 Most Important Thing today?   Yes ☐   No ☐

Today was awesome because _____

_____

Today I struggled with _____

_____

On a scale of 1–10, with 10 being the highest, I would rate today's productivity at a _____

Tomorrow I will...

Notes

_____

_____

_____

DAILY ACTION PLAN

MORNING ROUTINE

Hours Slept _____   Wake-up Time _____

Water ☐   Daily Journal ☐   _____ ☐   _____ ☐

This morning, I'm grateful for _____

GOALS AND M.I.N.S.

Goals are important to review daily, reinforcing your objectives to your conscious and subconscious mind. But goals alone are not enough. It's also vital that you take time to identify your Most Important Next Step (M.I.N.S.) for each goal, so your goal transforms into an action. And remember, when it comes to M.I.N.S., be specific.

GOAL #1 _____

Weekly Objective: _____

M.I.N.S. _____

GOAL #2 _____

Weekly Objective: _____

M.I.N.S. _____

GOAL #3 _____

Weekly Objective: _____

M.I.N.S. _____

I can consider today a "win" if I...

This is your #1 Most Important Thing!

TODAY'S TIME-BLOCKING ACTIVITIES

High-achievers know that what gets scheduled gets done. Take a few minutes to think about your goals, your M.I.N.S., and schedule your day. Don't forget to include several breaks.

5:00 _____	11:00 _____	5:00 _____
5:30 _____	11:30 _____	5:30 _____
6:00 _____	12:00 _____	6:00 _____
6:30 _____	12:30 _____	6:30 _____
7:00 _____	1:00 _____	7:00 _____
7:30 _____	1:30 _____	7:30 _____
8:00 _____	2:00 _____	8:00 _____
8:30 _____	2:30 _____	8:30 _____
9:00 _____	3:00 _____	9:00 _____
9:30 _____	3:30 _____	9:30 _____
10:00 _____	4:00 _____	10:00 _____
10:30 _____	4:30 _____	10:30 _____

☐ Did I include enough breaks in the day?   ☐ Did I schedule my #1 Most Important Thing?

EVENING REVIEW

Did you accomplish your #1 Most Important Thing today?   Yes ☐   No ☐

Today was awesome because _____

_____

Today I struggled with _____

_____

On a scale of 1–10, with 10 being the highest, I would rate today's productivity at a _____

Tomorrow I will...   Notes

_____   _____

_____   _____

_____   _____

DAILY ACTION PLAN

MORNING ROUTINE

Hours Slept _____   Wake-up Time _____

Water ☐   Daily Journal ☐   _____ ☐   _____ ☐

This morning, I'm grateful for _____

GOALS AND M.I.N.S.

Goals are important to review daily, reinforcing your objectives to your conscious and subconscious mind. But goals alone are not enough. It's also vital that you take time to identify your Most Important Next Step (M.I.N.S.) for each goal, so your goal transforms into an action. And remember, when it comes to M.I.N.S., be specific.

GOAL #1 _____

Weekly Objective: _____

M.I.N.S. _____

GOAL #2 _____

Weekly Objective: _____

M.I.N.S. _____

GOAL #3 _____

Weekly Objective: _____

M.I.N.S. _____

I can consider today a "win" if I...

This is your #1 Most Important Thing!

TODAY'S TIME-BLOCKING ACTIVITIES

High-achievers know that what gets scheduled gets done. Take a few minutes to think about your goals, your M.I.N.S., and schedule your day. Don't forget to include several breaks.

5:00 _____	11:00 _____	5:00 _____
5:30 _____	11:30 _____	5.30 _____
6:00 _____	12:00 _____	6:00 _____
6:30 _____	12:30 _____	6:30 _____
7:00 _____	1:00 _____	7:00 _____
7:30 _____	1:30 _____	7:30 _____
8:00 _____	2:00 _____	8:00 _____
8:30 _____	2:30 _____	8:30 _____
9:00 _____	3:00 _____	9:00 _____
9:30 _____	3:30 _____	9:30 _____
10:00 _____	4:00 _____	10:00 _____
10:30 _____	4:30 _____	10:30 _____

☐ Did I include enough breaks in the day?   ☐ Did I schedule my #1 Most Important Thing?

EVENING REVIEW

Did you accomplish your #1 Most Important Thing today?   Yes ☐   No ☐

Today was awesome because _____

_____

Today I struggled with _____

_____

On a scale of 1–10, with 10 being the highest, I would rate today's productivity at a _____

Tomorrow I will...   Notes

_____   _____

_____   _____

_____   _____

DAILY ACTION PLAN

MORNING ROUTINE

Hours Slept _____   Wake-up Time _____

Water ☐   Daily Journal ☐   _____ ☐   _____ ☐

This morning, I'm grateful for _____

GOALS AND M.I.N.S.

Goals are important to review daily, reinforcing your objectives to your conscious and subconscious mind. But goals alone are not enough. It's also vital that you take time to identify your Most Important Next Step (M.I.N.S.) for each goal, so your goal transforms into an action. And remember, when it comes to M.I.N.S., be specific.

GOAL #1 _____

Weekly Objective: _____

M.I.N.S. _____

GOAL #2 _____

Weekly Objective: _____

M.I.N.S. _____

GOAL #3 _____

Weekly Objective: _____

M.I.N.S. _____

I can consider today a "win" if I...

This is your #1 Most Important Thing!

TODAY'S TIME-BLOCKING ACTIVITIES

High-achievers know that what gets scheduled gets done. Take a few minutes to think about your goals, your M.I.N.S., and schedule your day. Don't forget to include several breaks.

5:00 _____	11:00 _____	5:00 _____
5:30 _____	11:30 _____	5:30 _____
6:00 _____	12:00 _____	6:00 _____
6:30 _____	12:30 _____	6:30 _____
7:00 _____	1:00 _____	7:00 _____
7:30 _____	1:30 _____	7:30 _____
8:00 _____	2:00 _____	8:00 _____
8:30 _____	2:30 _____	8:30 _____
9:00 _____	3:00 _____	9:00 _____
9:30 _____	3:30 _____	9:30 _____
10:00 _____	4:00 _____	10:00 _____
10:30 _____	4:30 _____	10:30 _____

☐ Did I include enough breaks in the day?

☐ Did I schedule my #1 Most Important Thing?

EVENING REVIEW

Did you accomplish your #1 Most Important Thing today?   Yes ☐   No ☐

Today was awesome because _____

_____

Today I struggled with _____

_____

On a scale of 1–10, with 10 being the highest, I would rate today's productivity at a _____

Tomorrow I will...

_____

_____

_____

Notes

_____

_____

_____

DAILY ACTION PLAN

MORNING ROUTINE

Hours Slept _____   Wake-up Time _____

Water ☐   Daily Journal ☐   _____ ☐   _____ ☐

This morning, I'm grateful for _____

GOALS AND M.I.N.S.

Goals are important to review daily, reinforcing your objectives to your conscious and subconscious mind. But goals alone are not enough. It's also vital that you take time to identify your Most Important Next Step (M.I.N.S.) for each goal, so your goal transforms into an action. And remember, when it comes to M.I.N.S., be specific.

GOAL #1 _____

Weekly Objective: _____

M.I.N.S. _____

GOAL #2 _____

Weekly Objective: _____

M.I.N.S. _____

GOAL #3 _____

Weekly Objective: _____

M.I.N.S. _____

I can consider today a "win" if I...

This is your #1 Most Important Thing!

TODAY'S TIME-BLOCKING ACTIVITIES

High-achievers know that what gets scheduled gets done. Take a few minutes to think about your goals, your M.I.N.S., and schedule your day. Don't forget to include several breaks.

5:00 _____	11:00 _____	5:00 _____
5:30 _____	11:30 _____	5:30 _____
6:00 _____	12:00 _____	6:00 _____
6:30 _____	12:30 _____	6:30 _____
7:00 _____	1:00 _____	7:00 _____
7:30 _____	1:30 _____	7:30 _____
8:00 _____	2:00 _____	8:00 _____
8:30 _____	2:30 _____	8:30 _____
9:00 _____	3:00 _____	9:00 _____
9:30 _____	3:30 _____	9:30 _____
10:00 _____	4:00 _____	10:00 _____
10:30 _____	4:30 _____	10:30 _____

☐ Did I include enough breaks in the day?

☐ Did I schedule my #1 Most Important Thing?

EVENING REVIEW

Did you accomplish your #1 Most Important Thing today? Yes ☐ No ☐

Today was awesome because _____

_____

Today I struggled with _____

_____

On a scale of 1–10, with 10 being the highest, I would rate today's productivity at a _____

Tomorrow I will...   Notes

_____   _____

_____   _____

_____   _____

DAILY ACTION PLAN

MORNING ROUTINE

Hours Slept _____   Wake-up Time _____

Water ☐   Daily Journal ☐   _____ ☐   _____ ☐

This morning, I'm grateful for _____

GOALS AND M.I.N.S.

Goals are important to review daily, reinforcing your objectives to your conscious and subconscious mind. But goals alone are not enough. It's also vital that you take time to identify your Most Important Next Step (M.I.N.S.) for each goal, so your goal transforms into an action. And remember, when it comes to M.I.N.S., be specific.

GOAL #1 _____

Weekly Objective: _____

M.I.N.S. _____

GOAL #2 _____

Weekly Objective: _____

M.I.N.S. _____

GOAL #3 _____

Weekly Objective: _____

M.I.N.S. _____

I can consider today a "win" if I...

This is your #1 Most Important Thing!

TODAY'S TIME-BLOCKING ACTIVITIES

High-achievers know that what gets scheduled gets done. Take a few minutes to think about your goals, your M.I.N.S., and schedule your day. Don't forget to include several breaks.

5:00 _____	11:00 _____	5:00 _____
5:30 _____	11:30 _____	5:30 _____
6:00 _____	12:00 _____	6:00 _____
6:30 _____	12:30 _____	6:30 _____
7:00 _____	1:00 _____	7:00 _____
7:30 _____	1:30 _____	7:30 _____
8:00 _____	2:00 _____	8:00 _____
8:30 _____	2:30 _____	8:30 _____
9:00 _____	3:00 _____	9:00 _____
9:30 _____	3:30 _____	9:30 _____
10:00 _____	4:00 _____	10:00 _____
10:30 _____	4:30 _____	10:30 _____

☐ Did I include enough breaks in the day?   ☐ Did I schedule my #1 Most Important Thing?

EVENING REVIEW

Did you accomplish your #1 Most Important Thing today?   Yes ☐   No ☐

Today was awesome because _____

_____

Today I struggled with _____

_____

On a scale of 1–10, with 10 being the highest, I would rate today's productivity at a _____

Tomorrow I will...   Notes

_____   _____

_____   _____

_____   _____

DAILY ACTION PLAN
MORNING ROUTINE

Hours Slept _____ Wake-up Time _____

Water ☐ Daily Journal ☐ _____ ☐ _____ ☐

This morning, I'm grateful for _____

GOALS AND M.I.N.S.

Goals are important to review daily, reinforcing your objectives to your conscious and subconscious mind. But goals alone are not enough. It's also vital that you take time to identify your Most Important Next Step (M.I.N.S.) for each goal, so your goal transforms into an action. And remember, when it comes to M.I.N.S., be specific.

GOAL #1 _____

Weekly Objective: _____

M.I.N.S. _____

GOAL #2 _____

Weekly Objective: _____

M.I.N.S. _____

GOAL #3 _____

Weekly Objective: _____

M.I.N.S. _____

I can consider today a "win" if I...

This is your #1 Most Important Thing!

TODAY'S TIME-BLOCKING ACTIVITIES

High-achievers know that what gets scheduled gets done. Take a few minutes to think about your goals, your M.I.N.S., and schedule your day. Don't forget to include several breaks.

5:00 _____	11:00 _____	5:00 _____
5:30 _____	11:30 _____	5:30 _____
6:00 _____	12:00 _____	6:00 _____
6:30 _____	12:30 _____	6:30 _____
7:00 _____	1:00 _____	7:00 _____
7:30 _____	1:30 _____	7:30 _____
8:00 _____	2:00 _____	8:00 _____
8:30 _____	2:30 _____	8:30 _____
9:00 _____	3:00 _____	9:00 _____
9:30 _____	3:30 _____	9:30 _____
10:00 _____	4:00 _____	10:00 _____
10:30 _____	4:30 _____	10:30 _____

☐ Did I include enough breaks in the day?   ☐ Did I schedule my #1 Most Important Thing?

EVENING REVIEW

Did you accomplish your #1 Most Important Thing today?   Yes ☐   No ☐

Today was awesome because _____

_____

Today I struggled with _____

_____

On a scale of 1–10, with 10 being the highest, I would rate today's productivity at a _____

Tomorrow I will...   Notes

_____   _____

_____   _____

_____   _____

DAILY ACTION PLAN

MORNING ROUTINE

Hours Slept _____   Wake-up Time _____

Water ☐   Daily Journal ☐   _____ ☐   _____ ☐

This morning, I'm grateful for _____

GOALS AND M.I.N.S.

Goals are important to review daily, reinforcing your objectives to your conscious and subconscious mind. But goals alone are not enough. It's also vital that you take time to identify your Most Important Next Step (M.I.N.S.) for each goal, so your goal transforms into an action. And remember, when it comes to M.I.N.S., be specific.

GOAL #1 _____

Weekly Objective: _____

M.I.N.S. _____

GOAL #2 _____

Weekly Objective: _____

M.I.N.S. _____

GOAL #3 _____

Weekly Objective: _____

M.I.N.S. _____

I can consider today a "win" if I...

This is your #1 Most Important Thing!

TODAY'S TIME-BLOCKING ACTIVITIES

High-achievers know that what gets scheduled gets done. Take a few minutes to think about your goals, your M.I.N.S., and schedule your day. Don't forget to include several breaks.

5:00 _____	11:00 _____	5:00 _____
5:30 _____	11:30 _____	5:30 _____
6:00 _____	12:00 _____	6:00 _____
6:30 _____	12:30 _____	6:30 _____
7:00 _____	1:00 _____	7:00 _____
7:30 _____	1:30 _____	7:30 _____
8:00 _____	2:00 _____	8:00 _____
8:30 _____	2:30 _____	8:30 _____
9:00 _____	3:00 _____	9:00 _____
9:30 _____	3:30 _____	9:30 _____
10:00 _____	4:00 _____	10:00 _____
10:30 _____	4:30 _____	10:30 _____

☐ Did I include enough breaks in the day?

☐ Did I schedule my #1 Most Important Thing?

EVENING REVIEW

Did you accomplish your #1 Most Important Thing today?   Yes ☐   No ☐

Today was awesome because _____

_____

Today I struggled with _____

_____

On a scale of 1–10, with 10 being the highest, I would rate today's productivity at a _____

Tomorrow I will...   Notes

_____   _____

_____   _____

_____   _____

DAILY ACTION PLAN

MORNING ROUTINE

Hours Slept _____   Wake-up Time _____

Water ☐   Daily Journal ☐   _____ ☐   _____ ☐

This morning, I'm grateful for _____

GOALS AND M.I.N.S.

Goals are important to review daily, reinforcing your objectives to your conscious and subconscious mind. But goals alone are not enough. It's also vital that you take time to identify your Most Important Next Step (M.I.N.S.) for each goal, so your goal transforms into an action. And remember, when it comes to M.I.N.S., be specific.

GOAL #1 _____

Weekly Objective: _____

M.I.N.S. _____

GOAL #2 _____

Weekly Objective: _____

M.I.N.S. _____

GOAL #3 _____

Weekly Objective: _____

M.I.N.S. _____

I can consider today a "win" if I...

This is your #1 Most Important Thing!

TODAY'S TIME-BLOCKING ACTIVITIES

High-achievers know that what gets scheduled gets done. Take a few minutes to think about your goals, your M.I.N.S., and schedule your day. Don't forget to include several breaks.

5:00	11:00	5:00
5:30	11:30	5:30
6:00	12:00	6:00
6:30	12:30	6:30
7:00	1:00	7:00
7:30	1:30	7:30
8:00	2:00	8:00
8:30	2:30	8:30
9:00	3:00	9:00
9:30	3:30	9:30
10:00	4:00	10:00
10:30	4:30	10:30

☐ Did I include enough breaks in the day?

☐ Did I schedule my #1 Most Important Thing?

EVENING REVIEW

Did you accomplish your #1 Most Important Thing today?   Yes ☐   No ☐

Today was awesome because _____

_____

Today I struggled with _____

_____

On a scale of 1–10, with 10 being the highest, I would rate today's productivity at a _____

Tomorrow I will...   Notes

_____   _____

_____   _____

_____   _____

DAILY ACTION PLAN

MORNING ROUTINE

Hours Slept _____   Wake-up Time _____

Water ☐   Daily Journal ☐   _____ ☐   _____ ☐

This morning, I'm grateful for _____

GOALS AND M.I.N.S.

Goals are important to review daily, reinforcing your objectives to your conscious and subconscious mind. But goals alone are not enough. It's also vital that you take time to identify your Most Important Next Step (M.I.N.S.) for each goal, so your goal transforms into an action. And remember, when it comes to M.I.N.S., be specific.

GOAL #1 _____

Weekly Objective: _____

M.I.N.S. _____

GOAL #2 _____

Weekly Objective: _____

M.I.N.S. _____

GOAL #3 _____

Weekly Objective: _____

M.I.N.S. _____

I can consider today a "win" if I...

This is your #1 Most Important Thing!

TODAY'S TIME-BLOCKING ACTIVITIES

High-achievers know that what gets scheduled gets done. Take a few minutes to think about your goals, your M.I.N.S., and schedule your day. Don't forget to include several breaks.

5:00 _____	11:00 _____	5:00 _____
5:30 _____	11:30 _____	5:30 _____
6:00 _____	12:00 _____	6:00 _____
6:30 _____	12:30 _____	6:30 _____
7:00 _____	1:00 _____	7:00 _____
7:30 _____	1:30 _____	7:30 _____
8:00 _____	2:00 _____	8:00 _____
8:30 _____	2:30 _____	8:30 _____
9:00 _____	3:00 _____	9:00 _____
9:30 _____	3:30 _____	9:30 _____
10:00 _____	4:00 _____	10:00 _____
10:30 _____	4:30 _____	10:30 _____

☐ Did I include enough breaks in the day?

☐ Did I schedule my #1 Most Important Thing?

EVENING REVIEW

Did you accomplish your #1 Most Important Thing today?   Yes ☐   No ☐

Today was awesome because _____

_____

Today I struggled with _____

_____

On a scale of 1–10, with 10 being the highest, I would rate today's productivity at a _____

Tomorrow I will...   Notes

_____   _____

_____   _____

_____   _____

DAILY ACTION PLAN

MORNING ROUTINE

Hours Slept _____   Wake-up Time _____

Water ☐   Daily Journal ☐   _____ ☐   _____ ☐

This morning, I'm grateful for _____

GOALS AND M.I.N.S.

Goals are important to review daily, reinforcing your objectives to your conscious and subconscious mind. But goals alone are not enough. It's also vital that you take time to identify your Most Important Next Step (M.I.N.S.) for each goal, so your goal transforms into an action. And remember, when it comes to M.I.N.S., be specific.

GOAL #1 _____

Weekly Objective: _____

M.I.N.S. _____

GOAL #2 _____

Weekly Objective: _____

M.I.N.S. _____

GOAL #3 _____

Weekly Objective: _____

M.I.N.S. _____

I can consider today a "win" if I...

This is your #1 Most Important Thing!

TODAY'S TIME-BLOCKING ACTIVITIES

High-achievers know that what gets scheduled gets done. Take a few minutes to think about your goals, your M.I.N.S., and schedule your day. Don't forget to include several breaks.

5:00 _____	11:00 _____	5:00 _____
5:30 _____	11:30 _____	5:30 _____
6:00 _____	12:00 _____	6:00 _____
6:30 _____	12:30 _____	6:30 _____
7:00 _____	1:00 _____	7:00 _____
7:30 _____	1:30 _____	7:30 _____
8:00 _____	2:00 _____	8:00 _____
8:30 _____	2:30 _____	8:30 _____
9:00 _____	3:00 _____	9:00 _____
9:30 _____	3:30 _____	9:30 _____
10:00 _____	4:00 _____	10:00 _____
10:30 _____	4:30 _____	10:30 _____

☐ Did I include enough breaks in the day?

☐ Did I schedule my #1 Most Important Thing?

EVENING REVIEW

Did you accomplish your #1 Most Important Thing today?   Yes ☐   No ☐

Today was awesome because _____

_____

Today I struggled with _____

_____

On a scale of 1–10, with 10 being the highest, I would rate today's productivity at a _____

Tomorrow I will...

Notes

DAILY ACTION PLAN

MORNING ROUTINE

Hours Slept _____   Wake-up Time _____

Water ☐   Daily Journal ☐   _____ ☐   _____ ☐

This morning, I'm grateful for _____

GOALS AND M.I.N.S.

Goals are important to review daily, reinforcing your objectives to your conscious and subconscious mind. But goals alone are not enough. It's also vital that you take time to identify your Most Important Next Step (M.I.N.S.) for each goal, so your goal transforms into an action. And remember, when it comes to M.I.N.S., be specific.

GOAL #1 _____

Weekly Objective: _____

M.I.N.S. _____

GOAL #2 _____

Weekly Objective: _____

M.I.N.S. _____

GOAL #3 _____

Weekly Objective: _____

M.I.N.S. _____

I can consider today a "win" if I...

This is your #1 Most Important Thing!

TODAY'S TIME-BLOCKING ACTIVITIES

High-achievers know that what gets scheduled gets done. Take a few minutes to think about your goals, your M.I.N.S., and schedule your day. Don't forget to include several breaks.

5:00 _____	11:00 _____	5:00 _____
5:30 _____	11:30 _____	5:30 _____
6:00 _____	12:00 _____	6:00 _____
6:30 _____	12:30 _____	6:30 _____
7:00 _____	1:00 _____	7:00 _____
7:30 _____	1:30 _____	7:30 _____
8:00 _____	2:00 _____	8:00 _____
8:30 _____	2:30 _____	8:30 _____
9:00 _____	3:00 _____	9:00 _____
9:30 _____	3:30 _____	9:30 _____
10:00 _____	4:00 _____	10:00 _____
10:30 _____	4:30 _____	10:30 _____

☐ Did I include enough breaks in the day?   ☐ Did I schedule my #1 Most Important Thing?

EVENING REVIEW

Did you accomplish your #1 Most Important Thing today?   Yes ☐   No ☐

Today was awesome because _____

_____

Today I struggled with _____

_____

On a scale of 1–10, with 10 being the highest, I would rate today's productivity at a _____

Tomorrow I will...   Notes

_____   _____

_____   _____

_____   _____

DAILY ACTION PLAN

MORNING ROUTINE

Hours Slept _____ Wake-up Time _____

Water ☐ Daily Journal ☐ _____ ☐ _____ ☐

This morning, I'm grateful for _____

GOALS AND M.I.N.S.

Goals are important to review daily, reinforcing your objectives to your conscious and subconscious mind. But goals alone are not enough. It's also vital that you take time to identify your Most Important Next Step (M.I.N.S.) for each goal, so your goal transforms into an action. And remember, when it comes to M.I.N.S., be specific.

GOAL #1 _____

Weekly Objective: _____

M.I.N.S. _____

GOAL #2 _____

Weekly Objective: _____

M.I.N.S. _____

GOAL #3 _____

Weekly Objective: _____

M.I.N.S. _____

I can consider today a "win" if I...

This is your #1 Most Important Thing!

TODAY'S TIME-BLOCKING ACTIVITIES

High-achievers know that what gets scheduled gets done. Take a few minutes to think about your goals, your M.I.N.S., and schedule your day. Don't forget to include several breaks.

5:00 _____	11:00 _____	5:00 _____
5:30 _____	11:30 _____	5:30 _____
6:00 _____	12:00 _____	6:00 _____
6:30 _____	12:30 _____	6:30 _____
7:00 _____	1:00 _____	7:00 _____
7:30 _____	1:30 _____	7:30 _____
8:00 _____	2:00 _____	8:00 _____
8:30 _____	2:30 _____	8:30 _____
9:00 _____	3:00 _____	9:00 _____
9:30 _____	3:30 _____	9:30 _____
10:00 _____	4:00 _____	10:00 _____
10:30 _____	4:30 _____	10:30 _____

☐ Did I include enough breaks in the day?　　　☐ Did I schedule my #1 Most Important Thing?

EVENING REVIEW

Did you accomplish your #1 Most Important Thing today?　Yes ☐　No ☐

Today was awesome because _____

_____

Today I struggled with _____

_____

On a scale of 1–10, with 10 being the highest, I would rate today's productivity at a _____

Tomorrow I will...　　　　　　　　　　　Notes

_____　　_____

_____　　_____

_____　　_____

DAILY ACTION PLAN

MORNING ROUTINE

Hours Slept _____ Wake-up Time _____

Water ☐ Daily Journal ☐ _____ ☐ _____ ☐

This morning, I'm grateful for _____

GOALS AND M.I.N.S.

Goals are important to review daily, reinforcing your objectives to your conscious and subconscious mind. But goals alone are not enough. It's also vital that you take time to identify your Most Important Next Step (M.I.N.S.) for each goal, so your goal transforms into an action. And remember, when it comes to M.I.N.S., be specific.

GOAL #1 _____

Weekly Objective: _____

M.I.N.S. _____

GOAL #2 _____

Weekly Objective: _____

M.I.N.S. _____

GOAL #3 _____

Weekly Objective: _____

M.I.N.S. _____

I can consider today a "win" if I...

This is your #1 Most Important Thing!

TODAY'S TIME-BLOCKING ACTIVITIES

High-achievers know that what gets scheduled gets done. Take a few minutes to think about your goals, your M.I.N.S., and schedule your day. Don't forget to include several breaks.

5:00 _____	11:00 _____	5:00 _____
5:30 _____	11:30 _____	5:30 _____
6:00 _____	12:00 _____	6:00 _____
6:30 _____	12:30 _____	6:30 _____
7:00 _____	1:00 _____	7:00 _____
7:30 _____	1:30 _____	7:30 _____
8:00 _____	2:00 _____	8:00 _____
8:30 _____	2:30 _____	8:30 _____
9:00 _____	3:00 _____	9:00 _____
9:30 _____	3:30 _____	9:30 _____
10:00 _____	4:00 _____	10:00 _____
10:30 _____	4:30 _____	10:30 _____

☐ Did I include enough breaks in the day?

☐ Did I schedule my #1 Most Important Thing?

EVENING REVIEW

Did you accomplish your #1 Most Important Thing today?   Yes ☐   No ☐

Today was awesome because _____

_____

Today I struggled with _____

_____

On a scale of 1–10, with 10 being the highest, I would rate today's productivity at a _____

Tomorrow I will...   Notes

_____   _____

_____   _____

_____   _____

DAILY ACTION PLAN

MORNING ROUTINE

Hours Slept _____ Wake-up Time _____

Water ☐   Daily Journal ☐   _____ ☐   _____ ☐

This morning, I'm grateful for _____

GOALS AND M.I.N.S.

Goals are important to review daily, reinforcing your objectives to your conscious and subconscious mind. But goals alone are not enough. It's also vital that you take time to identify your Most Important Next Step (M.I.N.S.) for each goal, so your goal transforms into an action. And remember, when it comes to M.I.N.S., be specific.

GOAL #1 _____

Weekly Objective: _____

M.I.N.S. _____

GOAL #2 _____

Weekly Objective: _____

M.I.N.S. _____

GOAL #3 _____

Weekly Objective: _____

M.I.N.S. _____

I can consider today a "win" if I...

This is your #1 Most Important Thing!

TODAY'S TIME-BLOCKING ACTIVITIES

High-achievers know that what gets scheduled gets done. Take a few minutes to think about your goals, your M.I.N.S., and schedule your day. Don't forget to include several breaks.

5:00 _____	11:00 _____	5:00 _____
5:30 _____	11:30 _____	5.30 _____
6:00 _____	12:00 _____	6:00 _____
6:30 _____	12:30 _____	6:30 _____
7:00 _____	1:00 _____	7:00 _____
7:30 _____	1:30 _____	7:30 _____
8:00 _____	2:00 _____	8:00 _____
8:30 _____	2:30 _____	8:30 _____
9:00 _____	3:00 _____	9:00 _____
9:30 _____	3:30 _____	9:30 _____
10:00 _____	4:00 _____	10:00 _____
10:30 _____	4:30 _____	10:30 _____

☐ Did I include enough breaks in the day?

☐ Did I schedule my #1 Most Important Thing?

EVENING REVIEW

Did you accomplish your #1 Most Important Thing today?   Yes ☐   No ☐

Today was awesome because _____

_____

Today I struggled with _____

_____

On a scale of 1–10, with 10 being the highest, I would rate today's productivity at a _____

Tomorrow I will...

Notes

_____   _____

_____   _____

_____   _____

DAILY ACTION PLAN
MORNING ROUTINE

Hours Slept _____   Wake-up Time _____

Water ☐   Daily Journal ☐   _____ ☐   _____ ☐

This morning, I'm grateful for _____

GOALS AND M.I.N.S.

Goals are important to review daily, reinforcing your objectives to your conscious and subconscious mind. But goals alone are not enough. It's also vital that you take time to identify your Most Important Next Step (M.I.N.S.) for each goal, so your goal transforms into an action. And remember, when it comes to M.I.N.S., be specific.

GOAL #1 _____

Weekly Objective: _____

M.I.N.S. _____

GOAL #2 _____

Weekly Objective: _____

M.I.N.S. _____

GOAL #3 _____

Weekly Objective: _____

M.I.N.S. _____

I can consider today a "win" if I...

This is your #1 Most Important Thing!

TODAY'S TIME-BLOCKING ACTIVITIES

High-achievers know that what gets scheduled gets done. Take a few minutes to think about your goals, your M.I.N.S., and schedule your day. Don't forget to include several breaks.

5:00 _____	11:00 _____	5:00 _____
5:30 _____	11:30 _____	5:30 _____
6:00 _____	12:00 _____	6:00 _____
6:30 _____	12:30 _____	6:30 _____
7:00 _____	1:00 _____	7:00 _____
7:30 _____	1:30 _____	7:30 _____
8:00 _____	2:00 _____	8:00 _____
8:30 _____	2:30 _____	8:30 _____
9:00 _____	3:00 _____	9:00 _____
9:30 _____	3:30 _____	9:30 _____
10:00 _____	4:00 _____	10:00 _____
10:30 _____	4:30 _____	10:30 _____

☐ Did I include enough breaks in the day?   ☐ Did I schedule my #1 Most Important Thing?

EVENING REVIEW

Did you accomplish your #1 Most Important Thing today?   Yes ☐   No ☐

Today was awesome because _____

_____

Today I struggled with _____

_____

On a scale of 1–10, with 10 being the highest, I would rate today's productivity at a _____

Tomorrow I will...   Notes

_____   _____

_____   _____

_____   _____

DAILY ACTION PLAN

MORNING ROUTINE

Hours Slept _____ Wake-up Time _____

Water ☐ Daily Journal ☐ _____ ☐ _____ ☐

This morning, I'm grateful for _____

GOALS AND M.I.N.S.

Goals are important to review daily, reinforcing your objectives to your conscious and subconscious mind. But goals alone are not enough. It's also vital that you take time to identify your Most Important Next Step (M.I.N.S.) for each goal, so your goal transforms into an action. And remember, when it comes to M.I.N.S., be specific.

GOAL #1 _____

Weekly Objective: _____

M.I.N.S. _____

GOAL #2 _____

Weekly Objective: _____

M.I.N.S. _____

GOAL #3 _____

Weekly Objective: _____

M.I.N.S. _____

I can consider today a "win" if I...

This is your #1 Most Important Thing!

TODAY'S TIME-BLOCKING ACTIVITIES

High-achievers know that what gets scheduled gets done. Take a few minutes to think about your goals, your M.I.N.S., and schedule your day. Don't forget to include several breaks.

5:00 _____	11:00 _____	5:00 _____
5:30 _____	11:30 _____	5:30 _____
6:00 _____	12:00 _____	6:00 _____
6:30 _____	12:30 _____	6:30 _____
7:00 _____	1:00 _____	7:00 _____
7:30 _____	1:30 _____	7:30 _____
8:00 _____	2:00 _____	8:00 _____
8:30 _____	2:30 _____	8:30 _____
9:00 _____	3:00 _____	9:00 _____
9:30 _____	3:30 _____	9:30 _____
10:00 _____	4:00 _____	10:00 _____
10:30 _____	4:30 _____	10:30 _____

☐ Did I include enough breaks in the day?

☐ Did I schedule my #1 Most Important Thing?

EVENING REVIEW

Did you accomplish your #1 Most Important Thing today?   Yes ☐   No ☐

Today was awesome because _____

_____

Today I struggled with _____

_____

On a scale of 1–10, with 10 being the highest, I would rate today's productivity at a _____

Tomorrow I will...   Notes

DAILY ACTION PLAN

MORNING ROUTINE

Hours Slept _____ Wake-up Time _____

Water ☐ Daily Journal ☐ _____ ☐ _____ ☐

This morning, I'm grateful for _____

GOALS AND M.I.N.S.

Goals are important to review daily, reinforcing your objectives to your conscious and subconscious mind. But goals alone are not enough. It's also vital that you take time to identify your Most Important Next Step (M.I.N.S.) for each goal, so your goal transforms into an action. And remember, when it comes to M.I.N.S., be specific.

GOAL #1 _____

Weekly Objective: _____

M.I.N.S. _____

GOAL #2 _____

Weekly Objective: _____

M.I.N.S. _____

GOAL #3 _____

Weekly Objective: _____

M.I.N.S. _____

I can consider today a "win" if I...

This is your #1 Most Important Thing!

TODAY'S TIME-BLOCKING ACTIVITIES

High-achievers know that what gets scheduled gets done. Take a few minutes to think about your goals, your M.I.N.S., and schedule your day. Don't forget to include several breaks.

5:00 ___	11:00 ___	5:00 ___
5:30 ___	11:30 ___	5:30 ___
6:00 ___	12:00 ___	6:00 ___
6:30 ___	12:30 ___	6:30 ___
7:00 ___	1:00 ___	7:00 ___
7:30 ___	1:30 ___	7:30 ___
8:00 ___	2:00 ___	8:00 ___
8:30 ___	2:30 ___	8:30 ___
9:00 ___	3:00 ___	9:00 ___
9:30 ___	3:30 ___	9:30 ___
10:00 ___	4:00 ___	10:00 ___
10:30 ___	4:30 ___	10:30 ___

☐ Did I include enough breaks in the day?

☐ Did I schedule my #1 Most Important Thing?

EVENING REVIEW

Did you accomplish your #1 Most Important Thing today?   Yes ☐   No ☐

Today was awesome because ___

___

Today I struggled with ___

___

On a scale of 1–10, with 10 being the highest, I would rate today's productivity at a ___

Tomorrow I will...   Notes

___   ___

___   ___

___

DAILY ACTION PLAN
MORNING ROUTINE

Hours Slept _____   Wake-up Time _____

Water ☐   Daily Journal ☐   _____ ☐   _____ ☐

This morning, I'm grateful for _____

GOALS AND M.I.N.S.

Goals are important to review daily, reinforcing your objectives to your conscious and subconscious mind. But goals alone are not enough. It's also vital that you take time to identify your Most Important Next Step (M.I.N.S.) for each goal, so your goal transforms into an action. And remember, when it comes to M.I.N.S., be specific.

GOAL #1 _____

Weekly Objective: _____

M.I.N.S. _____

GOAL #2 _____

Weekly Objective: _____

M.I.N.S. _____

GOAL #3 _____

Weekly Objective: _____

M.I.N.S. _____

I can consider today a "win" if I...

This is your #1 Most Important Thing!

TODAY'S TIME-BLOCKING ACTIVITIES

High-achievers know that what gets scheduled gets done. Take a few minutes to think about your goals, your M.I.N.S., and schedule your day. Don't forget to include several breaks.

5:00 _____	11:00 _____	5:00 _____
5:30 _____	11:30 _____	5:30 _____
6:00 _____	12:00 _____	6:00 _____
6:30 _____	12:30 _____	6:30 _____
7:00 _____	1:00 _____	7:00 _____
7:30 _____	1:30 _____	7:30 _____
8:00 _____	2:00 _____	8:00 _____
8:30 _____	2:30 _____	8:30 _____
9:00 _____	3:00 _____	9:00 _____
9:30 _____	3:30 _____	9:30 _____
10:00 _____	4:00 _____	10:00 _____
10:30 _____	4:30 _____	10:30 _____

☐ Did I include enough breaks in the day?

☐ Did I schedule my #1 Most Important Thing?

EVENING REVIEW

Did you accomplish your #1 Most Important Thing today?   Yes ☐   No ☐

Today was awesome because _____

_____

Today I struggled with _____

_____

On a scale of 1–10, with 10 being the highest, I would rate today's productivity at a _____

Tomorrow I will...   Notes

_____   _____

_____   _____

_____   _____

DAILY ACTION PLAN
MORNING ROUTINE

Hours Slept _____   Wake-up Time _____

Water ☐   Daily Journal ☐   _____ ☐   _____ ☐

This morning, I'm grateful for _____

GOALS AND M.I.N.S.

Goals are important to review daily, reinforcing your objectives to your conscious and subconscious mind. But goals alone are not enough. It's also vital that you take time to identify your Most Important Next Step (M.I.N.S.) for each goal, so your goal transforms into an action. And remember, when it comes to M.I.N.S., be specific.

GOAL #1 _____

Weekly Objective: _____

M.I.N.S. _____

GOAL #2 _____

Weekly Objective: _____

M.I.N.S. _____

GOAL #3 _____

Weekly Objective: _____

M.I.N.S. _____

I can consider today a "win" if I...

This is your #1 Most Important Thing!

TODAY'S TIME-BLOCKING ACTIVITIES

High-achievers know that what gets scheduled gets done. Take a few minutes to think about your goals, your M.I.N.S., and schedule your day. Don't forget to include several breaks.

5:00 _____	11:00 _____	5:00 _____
5:30 _____	11:30 _____	5:30 _____
6:00 _____	12:00 _____	6:00 _____
6:30 _____	12:30 _____	6:30 _____
7:00 _____	1:00 _____	7:00 _____
7:30 _____	1:30 _____	7:30 _____
8:00 _____	2:00 _____	8:00 _____
8:30 _____	2:30 _____	8:30 _____
9:00 _____	3:00 _____	9:00 _____
9:30 _____	3:30 _____	9:30 _____
10:00 _____	4:00 _____	10:00 _____
10:30 _____	4:30 _____	10:30 _____

☐ Did I include enough breaks in the day?

☐ Did I schedule my #1 Most Important Thing?

EVENING REVIEW

Did you accomplish your #1 Most Important Thing today?   Yes ☐   No ☐

Today was awesome because _____

_____

Today I struggled with _____

_____

On a scale of 1–10, with 10 being the highest, I would rate today's productivity at a _____

Tomorrow I will...

Notes

DAILY ACTION PLAN

MORNING ROUTINE

Hours Slept _____   Wake-up Time _____

Water ☐   Daily Journal ☐   _____ ☐   _____ ☐

This morning, I'm grateful for _____

GOALS AND M.I.N.S.

Goals are important to review daily, reinforcing your objectives to your conscious and subconscious mind. But goals alone are not enough. It's also vital that you take time to identify your Most Important Next Step (M.I.N.S.) for each goal, so your goal transforms into an action. And remember, when it comes to M.I.N.S., be specific.

GOAL #1 _____

Weekly Objective: _____

M.I.N.S. _____

GOAL #2 _____

Weekly Objective: _____

M.I.N.S. _____

GOAL #3 _____

Weekly Objective: _____

M.I.N.S. _____

I can consider today a "win" if I...

This is your #1 Most Important Thing!

TODAY'S TIME-BLOCKING ACTIVITIES

High-achievers know that what gets scheduled gets done. Take a few minutes to think about your goals, your M.I.N.S., and schedule your day. Don't forget to include several breaks.

5:00 _____	11:00 _____	5:00 _____
5:30 _____	11:30 _____	5:30 _____
6:00 _____	12:00 _____	6:00 _____
6:30 _____	12:30 _____	6:30 _____
7:00 _____	1:00 _____	7:00 _____
7:30 _____	1:30 _____	7:30 _____
8:00 _____	2:00 _____	8:00 _____
8:30 _____	2:30 _____	8:30 _____
9:00 _____	3:00 _____	9:00 _____
9:30 _____	3:30 _____	9:30 _____
10:00 _____	4:00 _____	10:00 _____
10:30 _____	4:30 _____	10:30 _____

☐ Did I include enough breaks in the day?

☐ Did I schedule my #1 Most Important Thing?

EVENING REVIEW

Did you accomplish your #1 Most Important Thing today?   Yes ☐   No ☐

Today was awesome because _____

_____

Today I struggled with _____

_____

On a scale of 1–10, with 10 being the highest, I would rate today's productivity at a _____

Tomorrow I will...   Notes

_____   _____

_____   _____

_____   _____

DAILY ACTION PLAN

MORNING ROUTINE

Hours Slept _____   Wake-up Time _____

Water ☐   Daily Journal ☐   _____ ☐   _____ ☐

This morning, I'm grateful for _____

GOALS AND M.I.N.S.

Goals are important to review daily, reinforcing your objectives to your conscious and subconscious mind. But goals alone are not enough. It's also vital that you take time to identify your Most Important Next Step (M.I.N.S.) for each goal, so your goal transforms into an action. And remember, when it comes to M.I.N.S., be specific.

GOAL #1 _____

Weekly Objective: _____

M.I.N.S. _____

GOAL #2 _____

Weekly Objective: _____

M.I.N.S. _____

GOAL #3 _____

Weekly Objective: _____

M.I.N.S. _____

I can consider today a "win" if I...

This is your #1 Most Important Thing!

TODAY'S TIME-BLOCKING ACTIVITIES

High-achievers know that what gets scheduled gets done. Take a few minutes to think about your goals, your M.I.N.S., and schedule your day. Don't forget to include several breaks.

5:00 _____	11:00 _____	5:00 _____
5:30 _____	11:30 _____	5:30 _____
6:00 _____	12:00 _____	6:00 _____
6:30 _____	12:30 _____	6:30 _____
7:00 _____	1:00 _____	7:00 _____
7:30 _____	1:30 _____	7:30 _____
8:00 _____	2:00 _____	8:00 _____
8:30 _____	2:30 _____	8:30 _____
9:00 _____	3:00 _____	9:00 _____
9:30 _____	3:30 _____	9:30 _____
10:00 _____	4:00 _____	10:00 _____
10:30 _____	4:30 _____	10:30 _____

☐ Did I include enough breaks in the day?

☐ Did I schedule my #1 Most Important Thing?

EVENING REVIEW

Did you accomplish your #1 Most Important Thing today?   Yes ☐   No ☐

Today was awesome because _____

_____

Today I struggled with _____

_____

On a scale of 1–10, with 10 being the highest, I would rate today's productivity at a _____

Tomorrow I will...   Notes

_____   _____

_____   _____

_____   _____

DAILY ACTION PLAN
MORNING ROUTINE

Hours Slept _____   Wake-up Time _____

Water ☐   Daily Journal ☐   _____ ☐   _____ ☐

This morning, I'm grateful for _____

GOALS AND M.I.N.S.

Goals are important to review daily, reinforcing your objectives to your conscious and subconscious mind. But goals alone are not enough. It's also vital that you take time to identify your Most Important Next Step (M.I.N.S.) for each goal, so your goal transforms into an action. And remember, when it comes to M.I.N.S., be specific.

GOAL #1 _____

Weekly Objective: _____

M.I.N.S. _____

GOAL #2 _____

Weekly Objective: _____

M.I.N.S. _____

GOAL #3 _____

Weekly Objective: _____

M.I.N.S. _____

I can consider today a "win" if I...

This is your #1 Most Important Thing!

TODAY'S TIME-BLOCKING ACTIVITIES

High-achievers know that what gets scheduled gets done. Take a few minutes to think about your goals, your M.I.N.S., and schedule your day. Don't forget to include several breaks.

5:00 _____	11:00 _____	5:00 _____
5:30 _____	11:30 _____	5:30 _____
6:00 _____	12:00 _____	6:00 _____
6:30 _____	12:30 _____	6:30 _____
7:00 _____	1:00 _____	7:00 _____
7:30 _____	1:30 _____	7:30 _____
8:00 _____	2:00 _____	8:00 _____
8:30 _____	2:30 _____	8:30 _____
9:00 _____	3:00 _____	9:00 _____
9:30 _____	3:30 _____	9:30 _____
10:00 _____	4:00 _____	10:00 _____
10:30 _____	4:30 _____	10:30 _____

☐ Did I include enough breaks in the day? ☐ Did I schedule my #1 Most Important Thing?

EVENING REVIEW

Did you accomplish your #1 Most Important Thing today?   Yes ☐   No ☐

Today was awesome because _____

_____

Today I struggled with _____

_____

On a scale of 1–10, with 10 being the highest, I would rate today's productivity at a _____

Tomorrow I will...   Notes

_____   _____

_____   _____

_____   _____

DAILY ACTION PLAN
MORNING ROUTINE

Hours Slept _____   Wake-up Time _____

Water ☐   Daily Journal ☐   _____ ☐   _____ ☐

This morning, I'm grateful for _____

GOALS AND M.I.N.S.

Goals are important to review daily, reinforcing your objectives to your conscious and subconscious mind. But goals alone are not enough. It's also vital that you take time to identify your Most Important Next Step (M.I.N.S.) for each goal, so your goal transforms into an action. And remember, when it comes to M.I.N.S., be specific.

GOAL #1 _____

Weekly Objective: _____

M.I.N.S. _____

GOAL #2 _____

Weekly Objective: _____

M.I.N.S. _____

GOAL #3 _____

Weekly Objective: _____

M.I.N.S. _____

I can consider today a "win" if I...

This is your #1 Most Important Thing!

TODAY'S TIME-BLOCKING ACTIVITIES

High-achievers know that what gets scheduled gets done. Take a few minutes to think about your goals, your M.I.N.S., and schedule your day. Don't forget to include several breaks.

5:00 _____	11:00 _____	5:00 _____
5:30 _____	11:30 _____	5:30 _____
6:00 _____	12:00 _____	6:00 _____
6:30 _____	12:30 _____	6:30 _____
7:00 _____	1:00 _____	7:00 _____
7:30 _____	1:30 _____	7:30 _____
8:00 _____	2:00 _____	8:00 _____
8:30 _____	2:30 _____	8:30 _____
9:00 _____	3:00 _____	9:00 _____
9:30 _____	3:30 _____	9:30 _____
10:00 _____	4:00 _____	10:00 _____
10:30 _____	4:30 _____	10:30 _____

☐ Did I include enough breaks in the day? ☐ Did I schedule my #1 Most Important Thing?

EVENING REVIEW

Did you accomplish your #1 Most Important Thing today? Yes ☐ No ☐

Today was awesome because _____

_____

Today I struggled with _____

_____

On a scale of 1–10, with 10 being the highest, I would rate today's productivity at a _____

Tomorrow I will...   Notes

_____   _____

_____   _____

_____   _____

DAILY ACTION PLAN
MORNING ROUTINE

Hours Slept _____   Wake-up Time _____

Water ☐   Daily Journal ☐   _____ ☐   _____ ☐

This morning, I'm grateful for _____

GOALS AND M.I.N.S.

Goals are important to review daily, reinforcing your objectives to your conscious and subconscious mind. But goals alone are not enough. It's also vital that you take time to identify your Most Important Next Step (M.I.N.S.) for each goal, so your goal transforms into an action. And remember, when it comes to M.I.N.S., be specific.

GOAL #1 _____

Weekly Objective: _____

M.I.N.S. _____

GOAL #2 _____

Weekly Objective: _____

M.I.N.S. _____

GOAL #3 _____

Weekly Objective: _____

M.I.N.S. _____

I can consider today a "win" if I...

This is your #1 Most Important Thing!

TODAY'S TIME-BLOCKING ACTIVITIES

High-achievers know that what gets scheduled gets done. Take a few minutes to think about your goals, your M.I.N.S., and schedule your day. Don't forget to include several breaks.

5:00	11:00	5:00
5:30	11:30	5:30
6:00	12:00	6:00
6:30	12:30	6:30
7:00	1:00	7:00
7:30	1:30	7:30
8:00	2:00	8:00
8:30	2:30	8:30
9:00	3:00	9:00
9:30	3:30	9:30
10:00	4:00	10:00
10:30	4:30	10:30

☐ Did I include enough breaks in the day?

☐ Did I schedule my #1 Most Important Thing?

EVENING REVIEW

Did you accomplish your #1 Most Important Thing today?   Yes ☐   No ☐

Today was awesome because _____

_____

Today I struggled with _____

_____

On a scale of 1–10, with 10 being the highest, I would rate today's productivity at a _____

Tomorrow I will...

Notes

DAILY ACTION PLAN
MORNING ROUTINE

Hours Slept _____   Wake-up Time _____

Water ☐   Daily Journal ☐   _____ ☐   _____ ☐

This morning, I'm grateful for _____

GOALS AND M.I.N.S.

Goals are important to review daily, reinforcing your objectives to your conscious and subconscious mind. But goals alone are not enough. It's also vital that you take time to identify your Most Important Next Step (M.I.N.S.) for each goal, so your goal transforms into an action. And remember, when it comes to M.I.N.S., be specific.

GOAL #1 _____

Weekly Objective: _____

M.I.N.S. _____

GOAL #2 _____

Weekly Objective: _____

M.I.N.S. _____

GOAL #3 _____

Weekly Objective: _____

M.I.N.S. _____

I can consider today a "win" if I...

This is your #1 Most Important Thing!

TODAY'S TIME-BLOCKING ACTIVITIES

High-achievers know that what gets scheduled gets done. Take a few minutes to think about your goals, your M.I.N.S., and schedule your day. Don't forget to include several breaks.

5:00 _____	11:00 _____	5:00 _____
5:30 _____	11:30 _____	5:30 _____
6:00 _____	12:00 _____	6:00 _____
6:30 _____	12:30 _____	6:30 _____
7:00 _____	1:00 _____	7:00 _____
7:30 _____	1:30 _____	7:30 _____
8:00 _____	2:00 _____	8:00 _____
8:30 _____	2:30 _____	8:30 _____
9:00 _____	3:00 _____	9:00 _____
9:30 _____	3:30 _____	9:30 _____
10:00 _____	4:00 _____	10:00 _____
10:30 _____	4:30 _____	10:30 _____

☐ Did I include enough breaks in the day?

☐ Did I schedule my #1 Most Important Thing?

EVENING REVIEW

Did you accomplish your #1 Most Important Thing today?   Yes ☐   No ☐

Today was awesome because _____

_____

Today I struggled with _____

_____

On a scale of 1–10, with 10 being the highest, I would rate today's productivity at a _____

Tomorrow I will...

Notes

DAILY ACTION PLAN
MORNING ROUTINE

Hours Slept _____ Wake-up Time _____

Water ☐ Daily Journal ☐ _____ ☐ _____ ☐

This morning, I'm grateful for _____

GOALS AND M.I.N.S.

Goals are important to review daily, reinforcing your objectives to your conscious and subconscious mind. But goals alone are not enough. It's also vital that you take time to identify your Most Important Next Step (M.I.N.S.) for each goal, so your goal transforms into an action. And remember, when it comes to M.I.N.S., be specific.

GOAL #1 _____

Weekly Objective: _____

M.I.N.S. _____

GOAL #2 _____

Weekly Objective: _____

M.I.N.S. _____

GOAL #3 _____

Weekly Objective: _____

M.I.N.S. _____

I can consider today a "win" if I...

This is your #1 Most Important Thing!

TODAY'S TIME-BLOCKING ACTIVITIES

High-achievers know that what gets scheduled gets done. Take a few minutes to think about your goals, your M.I.N.S., and schedule your day. Don't forget to include several breaks.

5:00 _____	11:00 _____	5:00 _____
5:30 _____	11:30 _____	5:30 _____
6:00 _____	12:00 _____	6:00 _____
6:30 _____	12:30 _____	6:30 _____
7:00 _____	1:00 _____	7:00 _____
7:30 _____	1:30 _____	7:30 _____
8:00 _____	2:00 _____	8:00 _____
8:30 _____	2:30 _____	8:30 _____
9:00 _____	3:00 _____	9:00 _____
9:30 _____	3:30 _____	9:30 _____
10:00 _____	4:00 _____	10:00 _____
10:30 _____	4:30 _____	10:30 _____

☐ Did I include enough breaks in the day?   ☐ Did I schedule my #1 Most Important Thing?

EVENING REVIEW

Did you accomplish your #1 Most Important Thing today?   Yes ☐   No ☐

Today was awesome because _____

_____

Today I struggled with _____

_____

On a scale of 1–10, with 10 being the highest, I would rate today's productivity at a _____

Tomorrow I will...   Notes

_____   _____

_____   _____

_____   _____

DAILY ACTION PLAN

MORNING ROUTINE

Hours Slept _____ Wake-up Time _____

Water ☐ Daily Journal ☐ _____ ☐ _____ ☐

This morning, I'm grateful for _____

GOALS AND M.I.N.S.

Goals are important to review daily, reinforcing your objectives to your conscious and subconscious mind. But goals alone are not enough. It's also vital that you take time to identify your Most Important Next Step (M.I.N.S.) for each goal, so your goal transforms into an action. And remember, when it comes to M.I.N.S., be specific.

GOAL #1 _____

Weekly Objective: _____

M.I.N.S. _____

GOAL #2 _____

Weekly Objective: _____

M.I.N.S. _____

GOAL #3 _____

Weekly Objective: _____

M.I.N.S. _____

I can consider today a "win" if I...

This is your #1 Most Important Thing!

TODAY'S TIME-BLOCKING ACTIVITIES

High-achievers know that what gets scheduled gets done. Take a few minutes to think about your goals, your M.I.N.S., and schedule your day. Don't forget to include several breaks.

5:00	11:00	5:00
5:30	11:30	5:30
6:00	12:00	6:00
6:30	12:30	6:30
7:00	1:00	7:00
7:30	1:30	7:30
8:00	2:00	8:00
8:30	2:30	8:30
9:00	3:00	9:00
9:30	3:30	9:30
10:00	4:00	10:00
10:30	4:30	10:30

☐ Did I include enough breaks in the day?

☐ Did I schedule my #1 Most Important Thing?

EVENING REVIEW

Did you accomplish your #1 Most Important Thing today?   Yes ☐   No ☐

Today was awesome because _____

_____

Today I struggled with _____

_____

On a scale of 1–10, with 10 being the highest, I would rate today's productivity at a _____

Tomorrow I will...

Notes

DAILY ACTION PLAN
MORNING ROUTINE

Hours Slept _____ Wake-up Time _____

Water ☐   Daily Journal ☐   _____ ☐   _____ ☐

This morning, I'm grateful for _____

GOALS AND M.I.N.S.

Goals are important to review daily, reinforcing your objectives to your conscious and subconscious mind. But goals alone are not enough. It's also vital that you take time to identify your Most Important Next Step (M.I.N.S.) for each goal, so your goal transforms into an action. And remember, when it comes to M.I.N.S., be specific.

GOAL #1 _____

Weekly Objective: _____

M.I.N.S. _____

GOAL #2 _____

Weekly Objective: _____

M.I.N.S. _____

GOAL #3 _____

Weekly Objective: _____

M.I.N.S. _____

I can consider today a "win" if I...

This is your #1 Most Important Thing!

TODAY'S TIME-BLOCKING ACTIVITIES

High-achievers know that what gets scheduled gets done. Take a few minutes to think about your goals, your M.I.N.S., and schedule your day. Don't forget to include several breaks.

5:00 _____	11:00 _____	5:00 _____
5:30 _____	11:30 _____	5:30 _____
6:00 _____	12:00 _____	6:00 _____
6:30 _____	12:30 _____	6:30 _____
7:00 _____	1:00 _____	7:00 _____
7:30 _____	1:30 _____	7:30 _____
8:00 _____	2:00 _____	8:00 _____
8:30 _____	2:30 _____	8:30 _____
9:00 _____	3:00 _____	9:00 _____
9:30 _____	3:30 _____	9:30 _____
10:00 _____	4:00 _____	10:00 _____
10:30 _____	4:30 _____	10:30 _____

☐ Did I include enough breaks in the day?

☐ Did I schedule my #1 Most Important Thing?

EVENING REVIEW

Did you accomplish your #1 Most Important Thing today?   Yes ☐   No ☐

Today was awesome because _____

_____

Today I struggled with _____

_____

On a scale of 1–10, with 10 being the highest, I would rate today's productivity at a _____

Tomorrow I will...   Notes

_____   _____

_____   _____

_____   _____

DAILY ACTION PLAN

MORNING ROUTINE

Hours Slept _____   Wake-up Time _____

Water ☐   Daily Journal ☐   _____ ☐   _____ ☐

This morning, I'm grateful for _____

GOALS AND M.I.N.S.

Goals are important to review daily, reinforcing your objectives to your conscious and subconscious mind. But goals alone are not enough. It's also vital that you take time to identify your Most Important Next Step (M.I.N.S.) for each goal, so your goal transforms into an action. And remember, when it comes to M.I.N.S., be specific.

GOAL #1 _____

Weekly Objective: _____

M.I.N.S. _____

GOAL #2 _____

Weekly Objective: _____

M.I.N.S. _____

GOAL #3 _____

Weekly Objective: _____

M.I.N.S. _____

I can consider today a "win" if I...

This is your #1 Most Important Thing!

TODAY'S TIME-BLOCKING ACTIVITIES

High-achievers know that what gets scheduled gets done. Take a few minutes to think about your goals, your M.I.N.S., and schedule your day. Don't forget to include several breaks.

5:00 _____	11:00 _____	5:00 _____
5:30 _____	11:30 _____	5:30 _____
6:00 _____	12:00 _____	6:00 _____
6:30 _____	12:30 _____	6:30 _____
7:00 _____	1:00 _____	7:00 _____
7:30 _____	1:30 _____	7:30 _____
8:00 _____	2:00 _____	8:00 _____
8:30 _____	2:30 _____	8:30 _____
9:00 _____	3:00 _____	9:00 _____
9:30 _____	3:30 _____	9:30 _____
10:00 _____	4:00 _____	10:00 _____
10:30 _____	4:30 _____	10:30 _____

☐ Did I include enough breaks in the day?

☐ Did I schedule my #1 Most Important Thing?

EVENING REVIEW

Did you accomplish your #1 Most Important Thing today?   Yes ☐   No ☐

Today was awesome because _____

_____

Today I struggled with _____

_____

On a scale of 1–10, with 10 being the highest, I would rate today's productivity at a _____

Tomorrow I will...

Notes

_____   _____

_____   _____

_____   _____

DAILY ACTION PLAN

MORNING ROUTINE

Hours Slept _____ Wake-up Time _____

Water ☐   Daily Journal ☐   _____ ☐   _____ ☐

This morning, I'm grateful for _____

GOALS AND M.I.N.S.

Goals are important to review daily, reinforcing your objectives to your conscious and subconscious mind. But goals alone are not enough. It's also vital that you take time to identify your Most Important Next Step (M.I.N.S.) for each goal, so your goal transforms into an action. And remember, when it comes to M.I.N.S., be specific.

GOAL #1 _____

Weekly Objective: _____

M.I.N.S. _____

GOAL #2 _____

Weekly Objective: _____

M.I.N.S. _____

GOAL #3 _____

Weekly Objective: _____

M.I.N.S. _____

I can consider today a "win" if I...

This is your #1 Most Important Thing!

TODAY'S TIME-BLOCKING ACTIVITIES

High-achievers know that what gets scheduled gets done. Take a few minutes to think about your goals, your M.I.N.S., and schedule your day. Don't forget to include several breaks.

5:00 _____	11:00 _____	5:00 _____
5:30 _____	11:30 _____	5:30 _____
6:00 _____	12:00 _____	6:00 _____
6:30 _____	12:30 _____	6:30 _____
7:00 _____	1:00 _____	7:00 _____
7:30 _____	1:30 _____	7:30 _____
8:00 _____	2:00 _____	8:00 _____
8:30 _____	2:30 _____	8:30 _____
9:00 _____	3:00 _____	9:00 _____
9:30 _____	3:30 _____	9:30 _____
10:00 _____	4:00 _____	10:00 _____
10:30 _____	4:30 _____	10:30 _____

☐ Did I include enough breaks in the day?

☐ Did I schedule my #1 Most Important Thing?

EVENING REVIEW

Did you accomplish your #1 Most Important Thing today? Yes ☐ No ☐

Today was awesome because _____

_____

Today I struggled with _____

_____

On a scale of 1–10, with 10 being the highest, I would rate today's productivity at a _____

Tomorrow I will...   Notes

_____   _____

_____   _____

_____   _____

DAILY ACTION PLAN
MORNING ROUTINE

Hours Slept _____ Wake-up Time _____

Water ☐ Daily Journal ☐ _____ ☐ _____ ☐

This morning, I'm grateful for _____

GOALS AND M.I.N.S.

Goals are important to review daily, reinforcing your objectives to your conscious and subconscious mind. But goals alone are not enough. It's also vital that you take time to identify your Most Important Next Step (M.I.N.S.) for each goal, so your goal transforms into an action. And remember, when it comes to M.I.N.S., be specific.

GOAL #1 _____

Weekly Objective: _____

M.I.N.S. _____

GOAL #2 _____

Weekly Objective: _____

M.I.N.S. _____

GOAL #3 _____

Weekly Objective: _____

M.I.N.S. _____

I can consider today a "win" if I...

This is your #1 Most Important Thing!

TODAY'S TIME-BLOCKING ACTIVITIES

High-achievers know that what gets scheduled gets done. Take a few minutes to think about your goals, your M.I.N.S., and schedule your day. Don't forget to include several breaks.

5:00 _____	11:00 _____	5:00 _____
5:30 _____	11:30 _____	5:30 _____
6:00 _____	12:00 _____	6:00 _____
6:30 _____	12:30 _____	6:30 _____
7:00 _____	1:00 _____	7:00 _____
7:30 _____	1:30 _____	7:30 _____
8:00 _____	2:00 _____	8:00 _____
8:30 _____	2:30 _____	8:30 _____
9:00 _____	3:00 _____	9:00 _____
9:30 _____	3:30 _____	9:30 _____
10:00 _____	4:00 _____	10:00 _____
10:30 _____	4:30 _____	10:30 _____

☐ Did I include enough breaks in the day?

☐ Did I schedule my #1 Most Important Thing?

EVENING REVIEW

Did you accomplish your #1 Most Important Thing today? Yes ☐ No ☐

Today was awesome because _____

_____

Today I struggled with _____

_____

On a scale of 1–10, with 10 being the highest, I would rate today's productivity at a _____

Tomorrow I will...   Notes

_____   _____

_____   _____

_____   _____

DAILY ACTION PLAN
MORNING ROUTINE

Hours Slept _____ Wake-up Time _____

Water ☐ Daily Journal ☐ _____ ☐ _____ ☐

This morning, I'm grateful for _____

GOALS AND M.I.N.S.

Goals are important to review daily, reinforcing your objectives to your conscious and subconscious mind. But goals alone are not enough. It's also vital that you take time to identify your Most Important Next Step (M.I.N.S.) for each goal, so your goal transforms into an action. And remember, when it comes to M.I.N.S., be specific.

GOAL #1 _____

Weekly Objective: _____

M.I.N.S. _____

GOAL #2 _____

Weekly Objective: _____

M.I.N.S. _____

GOAL #3 _____

Weekly Objective: _____

M.I.N.S. _____

I can consider today a "win" if I...

This is your #1 Most Important Thing!

TODAY'S TIME-BLOCKING ACTIVITIES

High-achievers know that what gets scheduled gets done. Take a few minutes to think about your goals, your M.I.N.S., and schedule your day. Don't forget to include several breaks.

5:00 _____	11:00 _____	5:00 _____
5:30 _____	11:30 _____	5:30 _____
6:00 _____	12:00 _____	6:00 _____
6:30 _____	12:30 _____	6:30 _____
7:00 _____	1:00 _____	7:00 _____
7:30 _____	1:30 _____	7:30 _____
8:00 _____	2:00 _____	8:00 _____
8:30 _____	2:30 _____	8:30 _____
9:00 _____	3:00 _____	9:00 _____
9:30 _____	3:30 _____	9:30 _____
10:00 _____	4:00 _____	10:00 _____
10:30 _____	4:30 _____	10:30 _____

☐ Did I include enough breaks in the day?   ☐ Did I schedule my #1 Most Important Thing?

EVENING REVIEW

Did you accomplish your #1 Most Important Thing today?   Yes ☐   No ☐

Today was awesome because _____

_____

Today I struggled with _____

_____

On a scale of 1–10, with 10 being the highest, I would rate today's productivity at a _____

Tomorrow I will...   Notes

_____   _____

_____   _____

_____   _____

DAILY ACTION PLAN
MORNING ROUTINE

Hours Slept _____ Wake-up Time _____

Water ☐ Daily Journal ☐ _____ ☐ _____ ☐

This morning, I'm grateful for _____

GOALS AND M.I.N.S.

Goals are important to review daily, reinforcing your objectives to your conscious and subconscious mind. But goals alone are not enough. It's also vital that you take time to identify your Most Important Next Step (M.I.N.S.) for each goal, so your goal transforms into an action. And remember, when it comes to M.I.N.S., be specific.

GOAL #1 _____

Weekly Objective: _____

M.I.N.S. _____

GOAL #2 _____

Weekly Objective: _____

M.I.N.S. _____

GOAL #3 _____

Weekly Objective: _____

M.I.N.S. _____

I can consider today a "win" if I...

This is your #1 Most Important Thing!

TODAY'S TIME-BLOCKING ACTIVITIES

High-achievers know that what gets scheduled gets done. Take a few minutes to think about your goals, your M.I.N.S., and schedule your day. Don't forget to include several breaks.

5:00 _____	11:00 _____	5:00 _____
5:30 _____	11:30 _____	5:30 _____
6:00 _____	12:00 _____	6:00 _____
6:30 _____	12:30 _____	6:30 _____
7:00 _____	1:00 _____	7:00 _____
7:30 _____	1:30 _____	7:30 _____
8:00 _____	2:00 _____	8:00 _____
8:30 _____	2:30 _____	8:30 _____
9:00 _____	3:00 _____	9:00 _____
9:30 _____	3:30 _____	9:30 _____
10:00 _____	4:00 _____	10:00 _____
10:30 _____	4:30 _____	10:30 _____

☐ Did I include enough breaks in the day?   ☐ Did I schedule my #1 Most Important Thing?

EVENING REVIEW

Did you accomplish your #1 Most Important Thing today?   Yes ☐   No ☐

Today was awesome because _____

_____

Today I struggled with _____

_____

On a scale of 1–10, with 10 being the highest, I would rate today's productivity at a _____

Tomorrow I will...   Notes

_____   _____

_____   _____

_____   _____

DAILY ACTION PLAN

MORNING ROUTINE

Hours Slept _____ Wake-up Time _____

Water ☐ Daily Journal ☐ _____ ☐ _____ ☐

This morning, I'm grateful for _____

GOALS AND M.I.N.S.

Goals are important to review daily, reinforcing your objectives to your conscious and subconscious mind. But goals alone are not enough. It's also vital that you take time to identify your Most Important Next Step (M.I.N.S.) for each goal, so your goal transforms into an action. And remember, when it comes to M.I.N.S., be specific.

GOAL #1 _____

Weekly Objective: _____

M.I.N.S. _____

GOAL #2 _____

Weekly Objective: _____

M.I.N.S. _____

GOAL #3 _____

Weekly Objective: _____

M.I.N.S. _____

I can consider today a "win" if I...

This is your #1 Most Important Thing!

TODAY'S TIME-BLOCKING ACTIVITIES

High-achievers know that what gets scheduled gets done. Take a few minutes to think about your goals, your M.I.N.S., and schedule your day. Don't forget to include several breaks.

5:00 _____	11:00 _____	5:00 _____
5:30 _____	11:30 _____	5:30 _____
6:00 _____	12:00 _____	6:00 _____
6:30 _____	12:30 _____	6:30 _____
7:00 _____	1:00 _____	7:00 _____
7:30 _____	1:30 _____	7:30 _____
8:00 _____	2:00 _____	8:00 _____
8:30 _____	2:30 _____	8:30 _____
9:00 _____	3:00 _____	9:00 _____
9:30 _____	3:30 _____	9:30 _____
10:00 _____	4:00 _____	10:00 _____
10:30 _____	4:30 _____	10:30 _____

☐ Did I include enough breaks in the day?

☐ Did I schedule my #1 Most Important Thing?

EVENING REVIEW

Did you accomplish your #1 Most Important Thing today? Yes ☐ No ☐

Today was awesome because _____

_____

Today I struggled with _____

_____

On a scale of 1–10, with 10 being the highest, I would rate today's productivity at a _____

Tomorrow I will...   Notes

_____   _____

_____   _____

_____   _____

DAILY ACTION PLAN

MORNING ROUTINE

Hours Slept _____   Wake-up Time _____

Water ☐   Daily Journal ☐   _____ ☐   _____ ☐

This morning, I'm grateful for _____

GOALS AND M.I.N.S.

Goals are important to review daily, reinforcing your objectives to your conscious and subconscious mind. But goals alone are not enough. It's also vital that you take time to identify your Most Important Next Step (M.I.N.S.) for each goal, so your goal transforms into an action. And remember, when it comes to M.I.N.S., be specific.

GOAL #1 _____

Weekly Objective: _____

M.I.N.S. _____

GOAL #2 _____

Weekly Objective: _____

M.I.N.S. _____

GOAL #3 _____

Weekly Objective: _____

M.I.N.S. _____

I can consider today a "win" if I...

This is your #1 Most Important Thing!

TODAY'S TIME-BLOCKING ACTIVITIES

High-achievers know that what gets scheduled gets done. Take a few minutes to think about your goals, your M.I.N.S., and schedule your day. Don't forget to include several breaks.

5:00 _____	11:00 _____	5:00 _____
5:30 _____	11:30 _____	5:30 _____
6:00 _____	12:00 _____	6:00 _____
6:30 _____	12:30 _____	6:30 _____
7:00 _____	1:00 _____	7:00 _____
7:30 _____	1:30 _____	7:30 _____
8:00 _____	2:00 _____	8:00 _____
8:30 _____	2:30 _____	8:30 _____
9:00 _____	3:00 _____	9:00 _____
9:30 _____	3:30 _____	9:30 _____
10:00 _____	4:00 _____	10:00 _____
10:30 _____	4:30 _____	10:30 _____

☐ Did I include enough breaks in the day?   ☐ Did I schedule my #1 Most Important Thing?

EVENING REVIEW

Did you accomplish your #1 Most Important Thing today?   Yes ☐   No ☐

Today was awesome because _____

_____

Today I struggled with _____

_____

On a scale of 1–10, with 10 being the highest, I would rate today's productivity at a _____

Tomorrow I will...   Notes

_____   _____

_____   _____

_____   _____

DAILY ACTION PLAN
MORNING ROUTINE

Hours Slept _____ Wake-up Time _____

Water ☐ Daily Journal ☐ _____ ☐ _____ ☐

This morning, I'm grateful for _____

GOALS AND M.I.N.S.

Goals are important to review daily, reinforcing your objectives to your conscious and subconscious mind. But goals alone are not enough. It's also vital that you take time to identify your Most Important Next Step (M.I.N.S.) for each goal, so your goal transforms into an action. And remember, when it comes to M.I.N.S., be specific.

GOAL #1 _____

Weekly Objective: _____

M.I.N.S. _____

GOAL #2 _____

Weekly Objective: _____

M.I.N.S. _____

GOAL #3 _____

Weekly Objective: _____

M.I.N.S. _____

I can consider today a "win" if I...

This is your #1 Most Important Thing!

TODAY'S TIME-BLOCKING ACTIVITIES

High-achievers know that what gets scheduled gets done. Take a few minutes to think about your goals, your M.I.N.S., and schedule your day. Don't forget to include several breaks.

5:00 _____	11:00 _____	5:00 _____
5:30 _____	11:30 _____	5:30 _____
6:00 _____	12:00 _____	6:00 _____
6:30 _____	12:30 _____	6:30 _____
7:00 _____	1:00 _____	7:00 _____
7:30 _____	1:30 _____	7:30 _____
8:00 _____	2:00 _____	8:00 _____
8:30 _____	2:30 _____	8:30 _____
9:00 _____	3:00 _____	9:00 _____
9:30 _____	3:30 _____	9:30 _____
10:00 _____	4:00 _____	10:00 _____
10:30 _____	4:30 _____	10:30 _____

☐ Did I include enough breaks in the day?   ☐ Did I schedule my #1 Most Important Thing?

EVENING REVIEW

Did you accomplish your #1 Most Important Thing today?   Yes ☐   No ☐

Today was awesome because _____

_____

Today I struggled with _____

_____

On a scale of 1–10, with 10 being the highest, I would rate today's productivity at a _____

Tomorrow I will...   Notes

_____   _____

_____   _____

_____   _____

DAILY ACTION PLAN

MORNING ROUTINE

Hours Slept _____ Wake-up Time _____

Water ☐ Daily Journal ☐ _____ ☐ _____ ☐

This morning, I'm grateful for _____

GOALS AND M.I.N.S.

Goals are important to review daily, reinforcing your objectives to your conscious and subconscious mind. But goals alone are not enough. It's also vital that you take time to identify your Most Important Next Step (M.I.N.S.) for each goal, so your goal transforms into an action. And remember, when it comes to M.I.N.S., be specific.

GOAL #1 _____

Weekly Objective: _____

M.I.N.S. _____

GOAL #2 _____

Weekly Objective: _____

M.I.N.S. _____

GOAL #3 _____

Weekly Objective: _____

M.I.N.S. _____

I can consider today a "win" if I...

This is your #1 Most Important Thing!

TODAY'S TIME-BLOCKING ACTIVITIES

High-achievers know that what gets scheduled gets done. Take a few minutes to think about your goals, your M.I.N.S., and schedule your day. Don't forget to include several breaks.

5:00 _____	11:00 _____	5:00 _____
5:30 _____	11:30 _____	5:30 _____
6:00 _____	12:00 _____	6:00 _____
6:30 _____	12:30 _____	6:30 _____
7:00 _____	1:00 _____	7:00 _____
7:30 _____	1:30 _____	7:30 _____
8:00 _____	2:00 _____	8:00 _____
8:30 _____	2:30 _____	8:30 _____
9:00 _____	3:00 _____	9:00 _____
9:30 _____	3:30 _____	9:30 _____
10:00 _____	4:00 _____	10:00 _____
10:30 _____	4:30 _____	10:30 _____

☐ Did I include enough breaks in the day?

☐ Did I schedule my #1 Most Important Thing?

EVENING REVIEW

Did you accomplish your #1 Most Important Thing today?   Yes ☐   No ☐

Today was awesome because _____

_____

Today I struggled with _____

_____

On a scale of 1–10, with 10 being the highest, I would rate today's productivity at a _____

Tomorrow I will...   Notes

_____   _____

_____   _____

_____   _____

DAILY ACTION PLAN

MORNING ROUTINE

Hours Slept _____ Wake-up Time _____

Water ☐ Daily Journal ☐ _____ ☐ _____ ☐

This morning, I'm grateful for _____

GOALS AND M.I.N.S.

Goals are important to review daily, reinforcing your objectives to your conscious and subconscious mind. But goals alone are not enough. It's also vital that you take time to identify your Most Important Next Step (M.I.N.S.) for each goal, so your goal transforms into an action. And remember, when it comes to M.I.N.S., be specific.

GOAL #1 _____

Weekly Objective: _____

M.I.N.S. _____

GOAL #2 _____

Weekly Objective: _____

M.I.N.S. _____

GOAL #3 _____

Weekly Objective: _____

M.I.N.S. _____

I can consider today a "win" if I...

This is your #1 Most Important Thing!

TODAY'S TIME-BLOCKING ACTIVITIES

High-achievers know that what gets scheduled gets done. Take a few minutes to think about your goals, your M.I.N.S., and schedule your day. Don't forget to include several breaks.

5:00 _____	11:00 _____	5:00 _____
5:30 _____	11:30 _____	5:30 _____
6:00 _____	12:00 _____	6:00 _____
6:30 _____	12:30 _____	6:30 _____
7:00 _____	1:00 _____	7:00 _____
7:30 _____	1:30 _____	7:30 _____
8:00 _____	2:00 _____	8:00 _____
8:30 _____	2:30 _____	8:30 _____
9:00 _____	3:00 _____	9:00 _____
9:30 _____	3:30 _____	9:30 _____
10:00 _____	4:00 _____	10:00 _____
10:30 _____	4:30 _____	10:30 _____

☐ Did I include enough breaks in the day?

☐ Did I schedule my #1 Most Important Thing?

EVENING REVIEW

Did you accomplish your #1 Most Important Thing today?　Yes ☐　No ☐

Today was awesome because _____

_____

Today I struggled with _____

_____

On a scale of 1–10, with 10 being the highest, I would rate today's productivity at a _____

Tomorrow I will...　　　　　　　　　Notes

_____　　　_____

_____　　　_____

_____　　　_____

DAILY ACTION PLAN
MORNING ROUTINE

Hours Slept _____ Wake-up Time _____

Water ☐ Daily Journal ☐ _____ ☐ _____ ☐

This morning, I'm grateful for _____

GOALS AND M.I.N.S.

Goals are important to review daily, reinforcing your objectives to your conscious and subconscious mind. But goals alone are not enough. It's also vital that you take time to identify your Most Important Next Step (M.I.N.S.) for each goal, so your goal transforms into an action. And remember, when it comes to M.I.N.S., be specific.

GOAL #1 _____

Weekly Objective: _____

M.I.N.S. _____

GOAL #2 _____

Weekly Objective: _____

M.I.N.S. _____

GOAL #3 _____

Weekly Objective: _____

M.I.N.S. _____

I can consider today a "win" if I...

This is your #1 Most Important Thing!

TODAY'S TIME-BLOCKING ACTIVITIES

High-achievers know that what gets scheduled gets done. Take a few minutes to think about your goals, your M.I.N.S., and schedule your day. Don't forget to include several breaks.

5:00 _____	11:00 _____	5:00 _____
5:30 _____	11:30 _____	5:30 _____
6:00 _____	12:00 _____	6:00 _____
6:30 _____	12:30 _____	6:30 _____
7:00 _____	1:00 _____	7:00 _____
7:30 _____	1:30 _____	7:30 _____
8:00 _____	2:00 _____	8:00 _____
8:30 _____	2:30 _____	8:30 _____
9:00 _____	3:00 _____	9:00 _____
9:30 _____	3:30 _____	9:30 _____
10:00 _____	4:00 _____	10:00 _____
10:30 _____	4:30 _____	10:30 _____

☐ Did I include enough breaks in the day?

☐ Did I schedule my #1 Most Important Thing?

EVENING REVIEW

Did you accomplish your #1 Most Important Thing today?   Yes ☐   No ☐

Today was awesome because _____

_____

Today I struggled with _____

_____

On a scale of 1–10, with 10 being the highest, I would rate today's productivity at a _____

Tomorrow I will...   Notes

_____   _____

_____   _____

_____   _____

DAILY ACTION PLAN

MORNING ROUTINE

Hours Slept _____   Wake-up Time _____

Water ☐   Daily Journal ☐   _____ ☐   _____ ☐

This morning, I'm grateful for _____

GOALS AND M.I.N.S.

Goals are important to review daily, reinforcing your objectives to your conscious and subconscious mind. But goals alone are not enough. It's also vital that you take time to identify your Most Important Next Step (M.I.N.S.) for each goal, so your goal transforms into an action. And remember, when it comes to M.I.N.S., be specific.

GOAL #1 _____

Weekly Objective: _____

M.I.N.S. _____

GOAL #2 _____

Weekly Objective: _____

M.I.N.S. _____

GOAL #3 _____

Weekly Objective: _____

M.I.N.S. _____

I can consider today a "win" if I...

This is your #1 Most Important Thing!

TODAY'S TIME-BLOCKING ACTIVITIES

High-achievers know that what gets scheduled gets done. Take a few minutes to think about your goals, your M.I.N.S., and schedule your day. Don't forget to include several breaks.

5:00 _____	11:00 _____	5:00 _____
5:30 _____	11:30 _____	5:30 _____
6:00 _____	12:00 _____	6:00 _____
6:30 _____	12:30 _____	6:30 _____
7:00 _____	1:00 _____	7:00 _____
7:30 _____	1:30 _____	7:30 _____
8:00 _____	2:00 _____	8:00 _____
8:30 _____	2:30 _____	8:30 _____
9:00 _____	3:00 _____	9:00 _____
9:30 _____	3:30 _____	9:30 _____
10:00 _____	4:00 _____	10:00 _____
10:30 _____	4:30 _____	10:30 _____

☐ Did I include enough breaks in the day?

☐ Did I schedule my #1 Most Important Thing?

EVENING REVIEW

Did you accomplish your #1 Most Important Thing today?   Yes ☐   No ☐

Today was awesome because _____

_____

Today I struggled with _____

_____

On a scale of 1–10, with 10 being the highest, I would rate today's productivity at a _____

Tomorrow I will...   Notes

_____   _____

_____   _____

_____   _____

JAN | FEB | MAR | APR | MAY | JUN | JUL | AUG | SEP | OCT | NOV | DEC
1 2 3 4 5 6 7 8 9 10 11 12 13 14 15 16 17 18 19 20 21 22 23 24 25 26 27 28 29 30 31

DAILY ACTION PLAN
MORNING ROUTINE

Hours Slept _____ Wake-up Time _____

Water ☐ Daily Journal ☐ _____ ☐ _____ ☐

This morning, I'm grateful for _____

GOALS AND M.I.N.S.

Goals are important to review daily, reinforcing your objectives to your conscious and subconscious mind. But goals alone are not enough. It's also vital that you take time to identify your Most Important Next Step (M.I.N.S.) for each goal, so your goal transforms into an action. And remember, when it comes to M.I.N.S., be specific.

GOAL #1 _____

Weekly Objective: _____

M.I.N.S. _____

GOAL #2 _____

Weekly Objective: _____

M.I.N.S. _____

GOAL #3 _____

Weekly Objective: _____

M.I.N.S. _____

I can consider today a "win" if I...

This is your #1 Most Important Thing!

TODAY'S TIME-BLOCKING ACTIVITIES

High-achievers know that what gets scheduled gets done. Take a few minutes to think about your goals, your M.I.N.S., and schedule your day. Don't forget to include several breaks.

5:00 _____	11:00 _____	5:00 _____
5:30 _____	11:30 _____	5:30 _____
6:00 _____	12:00 _____	6:00 _____
6:30 _____	12:30 _____	6:30 _____
7:00 _____	1:00 _____	7:00 _____
7:30 _____	1:30 _____	7:30 _____
8:00 _____	2:00 _____	8:00 _____
8:30 _____	2:30 _____	8:30 _____
9:00 _____	3:00 _____	9:00 _____
9:30 _____	3:30 _____	9:30 _____
10:00 _____	4:00 _____	10:00 _____
10:30 _____	4:30 _____	10:30 _____

☐ Did I include enough breaks in the day?

☐ Did I schedule my #1 Most Important Thing?

EVENING REVIEW

Did you accomplish your #1 Most Important Thing today?   Yes ☐   No ☐

Today was awesome because _____

_____

Today I struggled with _____

_____

On a scale of 1–10, with 10 being the highest, I would rate today's productivity at a _____

Tomorrow I will...   Notes

_____   _____

_____   _____

_____   _____

JAN | FEB | MAR | APR | MAY | JUN | JUL | AUG | SEP | OCT | NOV | DEC

1 2 3 4 5 6 7 8 9 10 11 12 13 14 15 16 17 18 19 20 21 22 23 24 25 26 27 28 29 30 31

DAILY ACTION PLAN
MORNING ROUTINE

Hours Slept _____ Wake-up Time _____

Water ☐ Daily Journal ☐ _____ ☐ _____ ☐

This morning, I'm grateful for _____

GOALS AND M.I.N.S.

Goals are important to review daily, reinforcing your objectives to your conscious and subconscious mind. But goals alone are not enough. It's also vital that you take time to identify your Most Important Next Step (M.I.N.S.) for each goal, so your goal transforms into an action. And remember, when it comes to M.I.N.S., be specific.

GOAL #1 _____

Weekly Objective: _____

M.I.N.S. _____

GOAL #2 _____

Weekly Objective: _____

M.I.N.S. _____

GOAL #3 _____

Weekly Objective: _____

M.I.N.S. _____

I can consider today a "win" if I...

This is your #1 Most Important Thing!

TODAY'S TIME-BLOCKING ACTIVITIES

High-achievers know that what gets scheduled gets done. Take a few minutes to think about your goals, your M.I.N.S., and schedule your day. Don't forget to include several breaks.

5:00	11:00	5:00
5:30	11:30	5:30
6:00	12:00	6:00
6:30	12:30	6:30
7:00	1:00	7:00
7:30	1:30	7:30
8:00	2:00	8:00
8:30	2:30	8:30
9:00	3:00	9:00
9:30	3:30	9:30
10:00	4:00	10:00
10:30	4:30	10:30

☐ Did I include enough breaks in the day?

☐ Did I schedule my #1 Most Important Thing?

EVENING REVIEW

Did you accomplish your #1 Most Important Thing today?   Yes ☐   No ☐

Today was awesome because _____

_____

Today I struggled with _____

_____

On a scale of 1–10, with 10 being the highest, I would rate today's productivity at a _____

Tomorrow I will...   Notes

DAILY ACTION PLAN
MORNING ROUTINE

Hours Slept _____ Wake-up Time _____

Water ☐ Daily Journal ☐ _____ ☐ _____ ☐

This morning, I'm grateful for _____

GOALS AND M.I.N.S.

Goals are important to review daily, reinforcing your objectives to your conscious and subconscious mind. But goals alone are not enough. It's also vital that you take time to identify your Most Important Next Step (M.I.N.S.) for each goal, so your goal transforms into an action. And remember, when it comes to M.I.N.S., be specific.

GOAL #1 _____

Weekly Objective: _____

M.I.N.S. _____

GOAL #2 _____

Weekly Objective: _____

M.I.N.S. _____

GOAL #3 _____

Weekly Objective: _____

M.I.N.S. _____

I can consider today a "win" if I...

This is your #1 Most Important Thing!

TODAY'S TIME-BLOCKING ACTIVITIES

High-achievers know that what gets scheduled gets done. Take a few minutes to think about your goals, your M.I.N.S., and schedule your day. Don't forget to include several breaks.

5:00 _____	11:00 _____	5:00 _____
5.30 _____	11:30 _____	5:30 _____
6:00 _____	12:00 _____	6:00 _____
6:30 _____	12:30 _____	6:30 _____
7:00 _____	1:00 _____	7:00 _____
7:30 _____	1:30 _____	7:30 _____
8:00 _____	2:00 _____	8:00 _____
8:30 _____	2:30 _____	8:30 _____
9:00 _____	3:00 _____	9:00 _____
9:30 _____	3:30 _____	9:30 _____
10:00 _____	4:00 _____	10:00 _____
10:30 _____	4:30 _____	10:30 _____

☐ Did I include enough breaks in the day?

☐ Did I schedule my #1 Most Important Thing?

EVENING REVIEW

Did you accomplish your #1 Most Important Thing today?   Yes ☐   No ☐

Today was awesome because _____

_____

Today I struggled with _____

_____

On a scale of 1–10, with 10 being the highest, I would rate today's productivity at a _____

Tomorrow I will...   Notes

_____   _____

_____   _____

_____   _____

DAILY ACTION PLAN
MORNING ROUTINE

Hours Slept _____ Wake-up Time _____

Water ☐ Daily Journal ☐ _____ ☐ _____ ☐

This morning, I'm grateful for _____

GOALS AND M.I.N.S.

Goals are important to review daily, reinforcing your objectives to your conscious and subconscious mind. But goals alone are not enough. It's also vital that you take time to identify your Most Important Next Step (M.I.N.S.) for each goal, so your goal transforms into an action. And remember, when it comes to M.I.N.S., be specific.

GOAL #1 _____

Weekly Objective: _____

M.I.N.S. _____

GOAL #2 _____

Weekly Objective: _____

M.I.N.S. _____

GOAL #3 _____

Weekly Objective: _____

M.I.N.S. _____

I can consider today a "win" if I...

This is your #1 Most Important Thing!

TODAY'S TIME-BLOCKING ACTIVITIES

High-achievers know that what gets scheduled gets done. Take a few minutes to think about your goals, your M.I.N.S., and schedule your day. Don't forget to include several breaks.

5:00 _____	11:00 _____	5:00 _____
5:30 _____	11:30 _____	5:30 _____
6:00 _____	12:00 _____	6:00 _____
6:30 _____	12:30 _____	6:30 _____
7:00 _____	1:00 _____	7:00 _____
7:30 _____	1:30 _____	7:30 _____
8:00 _____	2:00 _____	8:00 _____
8:30 _____	2:30 _____	8:30 _____
9:00 _____	3:00 _____	9:00 _____
9:30 _____	3:30 _____	9:30 _____
10:00 _____	4:00 _____	10:00 _____
10:30 _____	4:30 _____	10:30 _____

☐ Did I include enough breaks in the day?

☐ Did I schedule my #1 Most Important Thing?

EVENING REVIEW

Did you accomplish your #1 Most Important Thing today?   Yes ☐   No ☐

Today was awesome because _____

_____

Today I struggled with _____

_____

On a scale of 1–10, with 10 being the highest, I would rate today's productivity at a _____

Tomorrow I will...   Notes

_____   _____

_____   _____

_____   _____

DAILY ACTION PLAN
MORNING ROUTINE

Hours Slept _____ Wake-up Time _____

Water ☐ Daily Journal ☐ _____ ☐ _____ ☐

This morning, I'm grateful for _____

GOALS AND M.I.N.S.

Goals are important to review daily, reinforcing your objectives to your conscious and subconscious mind. But goals alone are not enough. It's also vital that you take time to identify your Most Important Next Step (M.I.N.S.) for each goal, so your goal transforms into an action. And remember, when it comes to M.I.N.S., be specific.

GOAL #1 _____

Weekly Objective: _____

M.I.N.S. _____

GOAL #2 _____

Weekly Objective: _____

M.I.N.S. _____

GOAL #3 _____

Weekly Objective: _____

M.I.N.S. _____

I can consider today a "win" if I...

This is your #1 Most Important Thing!

TODAY'S TIME-BLOCKING ACTIVITIES

High-achievers know that what gets scheduled gets done. Take a few minutes to think about your goals, your M.I.N.S., and schedule your day. Don't forget to include several breaks.

5:00 _____	11:00 _____	5:00 _____
5:30 _____	11:30 _____	5:30 _____
6:00 _____	12:00 _____	6:00 _____
6:30 _____	12:30 _____	6:30 _____
7:00 _____	1:00 _____	7:00 _____
7:30 _____	1:30 _____	7:30 _____
8:00 _____	2:00 _____	8:00 _____
8:30 _____	2:30 _____	8:30 _____
9:00 _____	3:00 _____	9:00 _____
9:30 _____	3:30 _____	9:30 _____
10:00 _____	4:00 _____	10:00 _____
10:30 _____	4:30 _____	10:30 _____

☐ Did I include enough breaks in the day?

☐ Did I schedule my #1 Most Important Thing?

EVENING REVIEW

Did you accomplish your #1 Most Important Thing today?   Yes ☐   No ☐

Today was awesome because _____

_____

Today I struggled with _____

_____

On a scale of 1–10, with 10 being the highest, I would rate today's productivity at a _____

Tomorrow I will...   Notes

_____   _____

_____   _____

_____   _____

DAILY ACTION PLAN
MORNING ROUTINE

Hours Slept _____   Wake-up Time _____

Water ☐   Daily Journal ☐   _____ ☐ _____ ☐

This morning, I'm grateful for _____

GOALS AND M.I.N.S.

Goals are important to review daily, reinforcing your objectives to your conscious and subconscious mind. But goals alone are not enough. It's also vital that you take time to identify your Most Important Next Step (M.I.N.S.) for each goal, so your goal transforms into an action. And remember, when it comes to M.I.N.S., be specific.

GOAL #1 _____

Weekly Objective: _____

M.I.N.S. _____

GOAL #2 _____

Weekly Objective: _____

M.I.N.S. _____

GOAL #3 _____

Weekly Objective: _____

M.I.N.S. _____

I can consider today a "win" if I...

This is your #1 Most Important Thing!

TODAY'S TIME-BLOCKING ACTIVITIES

High-achievers know that what gets scheduled gets done. Take a few minutes to think about your goals, your M.I.N.S., and schedule your day. Don't forget to include several breaks.

5:00 _____	11:00 _____	5:00 _____
5:30 _____	11:30 _____	5:30 _____
6:00 _____	12:00 _____	6:00 _____
6:30 _____	12:30 _____	6:30 _____
7:00 _____	1:00 _____	7:00 _____
7:30 _____	1:30 _____	7:30 _____
8:00 _____	2:00 _____	8:00 _____
8:30 _____	2:30 _____	8:30 _____
9:00 _____	3:00 _____	9:00 _____
9:30 _____	3:30 _____	9:30 _____
10:00 _____	4:00 _____	10:00 _____
10:30 _____	4:30 _____	10:30 _____

☐ Did I include enough breaks in the day?   ☐ Did I schedule my #1 Most Important Thing?

EVENING REVIEW

Did you accomplish your #1 Most Important Thing today?   Yes ☐   No ☐

Today was awesome because _____

_____

Today I struggled with _____

_____

On a scale of 1–10, with 10 being the highest, I would rate today's productivity at a _____

Tomorrow I will...   Notes

_____   _____

_____   _____

_____   _____

JAN | FEB | MAR | APR | MAY | JUN | JUL | AUG | SEP | OCT | NOV | DEC

1 2 3 4 5 6 7 8 9 10 11 12 13 14 15 16 17 18 19 20 21 22 23 24 25 26 27 28 29 30 31

DAILY ACTION PLAN
MORNING ROUTINE

Hours Slept _____ Wake-up Time _____

Water ☐ Daily Journal ☐ _____ ☐ _____ ☐

This morning, I'm grateful for _____

GOALS AND M.I.N.S.

Goals are important to review daily, reinforcing your objectives to your conscious and subconscious mind. But goals alone are not enough. It's also vital that you take time to identify your Most Important Next Step (M.I.N.S.) for each goal, so your goal transforms into an action. And remember, when it comes to M.I.N.S., be specific.

GOAL #1 _____

Weekly Objective: _____

M.I.N.S. _____

GOAL #2 _____

Weekly Objective: _____

M.I.N.S. _____

GOAL #3 _____

Weekly Objective: _____

M.I.N.S. _____

I can consider today a "win" if I...

This is your #1 Most Important Thing!

TODAY'S TIME-BLOCKING ACTIVITIES

High-achievers know that what gets scheduled gets done. Take a few minutes to think about your goals, your M.I.N.S., and schedule your day. Don't forget to include several breaks.

5:00 _____	11:00 _____	5:00 _____
5:30 _____	11:30 _____	5:30 _____
6:00 _____	12:00 _____	6:00 _____
6:30 _____	12:30 _____	6:30 _____
7:00 _____	1:00 _____	7:00 _____
7:30 _____	1:30 _____	7:30 _____
8:00 _____	2:00 _____	8:00 _____
8:30 _____	2:30 _____	8:30 _____
9:00 _____	3:00 _____	9:00 _____
9:30 _____	3:30 _____	9:30 _____
10:00 _____	4:00 _____	10:00 _____
10:30 _____	4:30 _____	10:30 _____

☐ Did I include enough breaks in the day?

☐ Did I schedule my #1 Most Important Thing?

EVENING REVIEW

Did you accomplish your #1 Most Important Thing today? Yes ☐ No ☐

Today was awesome because _____

_____

Today I struggled with _____

_____

On a scale of 1–10, with 10 being the highest, I would rate today's productivity at a _____

Tomorrow I will...   Notes

_____   _____

_____   _____

_____   _____

DAILY ACTION PLAN
MORNING ROUTINE

Hours Slept _____ Wake-up Time _____

Water ☐ Daily Journal ☐ _____ ☐ _____ ☐

This morning, I'm grateful for _____

GOALS AND M.I.N.S.

Goals are important to review daily, reinforcing your objectives to your conscious and subconscious mind. But goals alone are not enough. It's also vital that you take time to identify your Most Important Next Step (M.I.N.S.) for each goal, so your goal transforms into an action. And remember, when it comes to M.I.N.S., be specific.

GOAL #1 _____

Weekly Objective: _____

M.I.N.S. _____

GOAL #2 _____

Weekly Objective: _____

M.I.N.S. _____

GOAL #3 _____

Weekly Objective: _____

M.I.N.S. _____

I can consider today a "win" if I...

This is your #1 Most Important Thing!

TODAY'S TIME-BLOCKING ACTIVITIES

High-achievers know that what gets scheduled gets done. Take a few minutes to think about your goals, your M.I.N.S., and schedule your day. Don't forget to include several breaks.

5:00	11:00	5:00
5:30	11:30	5:30
6:00	12:00	6:00
6:30	12:30	6:30
7:00	1:00	7:00
7:30	1:30	7:30
8:00	2:00	8:00
8:30	2:30	8:30
9:00	3:00	9:00
9:30	3:30	9:30
10:00	4:00	10:00
10:30	4:30	10:30

☐ Did I include enough breaks in the day?

☐ Did I schedule my #1 Most Important Thing?

EVENING REVIEW

Did you accomplish your #1 Most Important Thing today?   Yes ☐   No ☐

Today was awesome because _____

_____

Today I struggled with _____

_____

On a scale of 1–10, with 10 being the highest, I would rate today's productivity at a _____

Tomorrow I will...

Notes

DAILY ACTION PLAN
MORNING ROUTINE

Hours Slept _____ Wake-up Time _____

Water ☐ Daily Journal ☐ _____ ☐ _____ ☐

This morning, I'm grateful for _____

GOALS AND M.I.N.S.

Goals are important to review daily, reinforcing your objectives to your conscious and subconscious mind. But goals alone are not enough. It's also vital that you take time to identify your Most Important Next Step (M.I.N.S.) for each goal, so your goal transforms into an action. And remember, when it comes to M.I.N.S., be specific.

GOAL #1 _____

Weekly Objective: _____

M.I.N.S. _____

GOAL #2 _____

Weekly Objective: _____

M.I.N.S. _____

GOAL #3 _____

Weekly Objective: _____

M.I.N.S. _____

I can consider today a "win" if I...

This is your #1 Most Important Thing!

TODAY'S TIME-BLOCKING ACTIVITIES

High-achievers know that what gets scheduled gets done. Take a few minutes to think about your goals, your M.I.N.S., and schedule your day. Don't forget to include several breaks.

5:00 _____	11:00 _____	5:00 _____
5:30 _____	11:30 _____	5:30 _____
6:00 _____	12:00 _____	6:00 _____
6:30 _____	12:30 _____	6:30 _____
7:00 _____	1:00 _____	7:00 _____
7:30 _____	1:30 _____	7:30 _____
8:00 _____	2:00 _____	8:00 _____
8:30 _____	2:30 _____	8:30 _____
9:00 _____	3:00 _____	9:00 _____
9:30 _____	3:30 _____	9:30 _____
10:00 _____	4:00 _____	10:00 _____
10:30 _____	4:30 _____	10:30 _____

☐ Did I include enough breaks in the day?

☐ Did I schedule my #1 Most Important Thing?

EVENING REVIEW

Did you accomplish your #1 Most Important Thing today?   Yes ☐   No ☐

Today was awesome because _____

_____

Today I struggled with _____

_____

On a scale of 1–10, with 10 being the highest, I would rate today's productivity at a _____

Tomorrow I will...

Notes

DAILY ACTION PLAN

MORNING ROUTINE

Hours Slept _____   Wake-up Time _____

Water ☐   Daily Journal ☐   _____ ☐   _____ ☐

This morning, I'm grateful for _____

GOALS AND M.I.N.S.

Goals are important to review daily, reinforcing your objectives to your conscious and subconscious mind. But goals alone are not enough. It's also vital that you take time to identify your Most Important Next Step (M.I.N.S.) for each goal, so your goal transforms into an action. And remember, when it comes to M.I.N.S., be specific.

GOAL #1 _____

Weekly Objective: _____

M.I.N.S. _____

GOAL #2 _____

Weekly Objective: _____

M.I.N.S. _____

GOAL #3 _____

Weekly Objective: _____

M.I.N.S. _____

I can consider today a "win" if I...

This is your #1 Most Important Thing!

TODAY'S TIME-BLOCKING ACTIVITIES

High-achievers know that what gets scheduled gets done. Take a few minutes to think about your goals, your M.I.N.S., and schedule your day. Don't forget to include several breaks.

5:00	11:00	5:00
5:30	11:30	5:30
6:00	12:00	6:00
6:30	12:30	6:30
7:00	1:00	7:00
7:30	1:30	7:30
8:00	2:00	8:00
8:30	2:30	8:30
9:00	3:00	9:00
9:30	3:30	9:30
10:00	4:00	10:00
10:30	4:30	10:30

☐ Did I include enough breaks in the day?

☐ Did I schedule my #1 Most Important Thing?

EVENING REVIEW

Did you accomplish your #1 Most Important Thing today?   Yes ☐   No ☐

Today was awesome because _____

_____

Today I struggled with _____

_____

On a scale of 1–10, with 10 being the highest, I would rate today's productivity at a _____

Tomorrow I will...   Notes

DAILY ACTION PLAN

MORNING ROUTINE

Hours Slept _____ Wake-up Time _____

Water ☐ Daily Journal ☐ _____ ☐ _____ ☐

This morning, I'm grateful for _____

GOALS AND M.I.N.S.

Goals are important to review daily, reinforcing your objectives to your conscious and subconscious mind. But goals alone are not enough. It's also vital that you take time to identify your Most Important Next Step (M.I.N.S.) for each goal, so your goal transforms into an action. And remember, when it comes to M.I.N.S., be specific.

GOAL #1 _____

Weekly Objective: _____

M.I.N.S. _____

GOAL #2 _____

Weekly Objective: _____

M.I.N.S. _____

GOAL #3 _____

Weekly Objective: _____

M.I.N.S. _____

I can consider today a "win" if I...

This is your #1 Most Important Thing!

TODAY'S TIME-BLOCKING ACTIVITIES

High-achievers know that what gets scheduled gets done. Take a few minutes to think about your goals, your M.I.N.S., and schedule your day. Don't forget to include several breaks.

5:00 _____	11:00 _____	5:00 _____
5:30 _____	11:30 _____	5:30 _____
6:00 _____	12:00 _____	6:00 _____
6:30 _____	12:30 _____	6:30 _____
7:00 _____	1:00 _____	7:00 _____
7:30 _____	1:30 _____	7:30 _____
8:00 _____	2:00 _____	8:00 _____
8:30 _____	2:30 _____	8:30 _____
9:00 _____	3:00 _____	9:00 _____
9:30 _____	3:30 _____	9:30 _____
10:00 _____	4:00 _____	10:00 _____
10:30 _____	4:30 _____	10:30 _____

☐ Did I include enough breaks in the day?

☐ Did I schedule my #1 Most Important Thing?

EVENING REVIEW

Did you accomplish your #1 Most Important Thing today? Yes ☐ No ☐

Today was awesome because _____

_____

Today I struggled with _____

_____

On a scale of 1–10, with 10 being the highest, I would rate today's productivity at a _____

Tomorrow I will...   Notes

_____   _____

_____   _____

_____   _____

DAILY ACTION PLAN
MORNING ROUTINE

Hours Slept _____   Wake-up Time _____

Water ☐   Daily Journal ☐   _____ ☐   _____ ☐

This morning, I'm grateful for _____

GOALS AND M.I.N.S.

Goals are important to review daily, reinforcing your objectives to your conscious and subconscious mind. But goals alone are not enough. It's also vital that you take time to identify your Most Important Next Step (M.I.N.S.) for each goal, so your goal transforms into an action. And remember, when it comes to M.I.N.S., be specific.

GOAL #1 _____

Weekly Objective: _____

M.I.N.S. _____

GOAL #2 _____

Weekly Objective: _____

M.I.N.S. _____

GOAL #3 _____

Weekly Objective: _____

M.I.N.S. _____

I can consider today a "win" if I...

This is your #1 Most Important Thing!

TODAY'S TIME-BLOCKING ACTIVITIES

High-achievers know that what gets scheduled gets done. Take a few minutes to think about your goals, your M.I.N.S., and schedule your day. Don't forget to include several breaks.

5:00 _____	11:00 _____	5:00 _____
5:30 _____	11:30 _____	5:30 _____
6:00 _____	12:00 _____	6:00 _____
6:30 _____	12:30 _____	6:30 _____
7:00 _____	1:00 _____	7:00 _____
7:30 _____	1:30 _____	7:30 _____
8:00 _____	2:00 _____	8:00 _____
8:30 _____	2:30 _____	8:30 _____
9:00 _____	3:00 _____	9:00 _____
9:30 _____	3:30 _____	9:30 _____
10:00 _____	4:00 _____	10:00 _____
10:30 _____	4:30 _____	10:30 _____

☐ Did I include enough breaks in the day?

☐ Did I schedule my #1 Most Important Thing?

EVENING REVIEW

Did you accomplish your #1 Most Important Thing today?   Yes ☐   No ☐

Today was awesome because _____

_____

Today I struggled with _____

_____

On a scale of 1–10, with 10 being the highest, I would rate today's productivity at a _____

Tomorrow I will...

Notes

_____ | _____

_____ | _____

_____ | _____

DAILY ACTION PLAN
MORNING ROUTINE

Hours Slept _____   Wake-up Time _____

Water ☐   Daily Journal ☐   _____ ☐   _____ ☐

This morning, I'm grateful for _____

GOALS AND M.I.N.S.

Goals are important to review daily, reinforcing your objectives to your conscious and subconscious mind. But goals alone are not enough. It's also vital that you take time to identify your Most Important Next Step (M.I.N.S.) for each goal, so your goal transforms into an action. And remember, when it comes to M.I.N.S., be specific.

GOAL #1 _____

Weekly Objective: _____

M.I.N.S. _____

GOAL #2 _____

Weekly Objective: _____

M.I.N.S. _____

GOAL #3 _____

Weekly Objective: _____

M.I.N.S. _____

I can consider today a "win" if I...

This is your #1 Most Important Thing!

TODAY'S TIME-BLOCKING ACTIVITIES

High-achievers know that what gets scheduled gets done. Take a few minutes to think about your goals, your M.I.N.S., and schedule your day. Don't forget to include several breaks.

5:00 _____	11:00 _____	5:00 _____
5:30 _____	11:30 _____	5:30 _____
6:00 _____	12:00 _____	6:00 _____
6:30 _____	12:30 _____	6:30 _____
7:00 _____	1:00 _____	7:00 _____
7:30 _____	1:30 _____	7:30 _____
8:00 _____	2:00 _____	8:00 _____
8:30 _____	2:30 _____	8:30 _____
9:00 _____	3:00 _____	9:00 _____
9:30 _____	3:30 _____	9:30 _____
10:00 _____	4:00 _____	10:00 _____
10:30 _____	4:30 _____	10:30 _____

☐ Did I include enough breaks in the day?

☐ Did I schedule my #1 Most Important Thing?

EVENING REVIEW

Did you accomplish your #1 Most Important Thing today?   Yes ☐   No ☐

Today was awesome because _____

_____

Today I struggled with _____

_____

On a scale of 1–10, with 10 being the highest, I would rate today's productivity at a _____

Tomorrow I will...

_____

_____

_____

Notes

_____

_____

_____

DAILY ACTION PLAN

MORNING ROUTINE

Hours Slept _____ Wake-up Time _____

Water ☐ Daily Journal ☐ _____ ☐ _____ ☐

This morning, I'm grateful for _____

GOALS AND M.I.N.S.

Goals are important to review daily, reinforcing your objectives to your conscious and subconscious mind. But goals alone are not enough. It's also vital that you take time to identify your Most Important Next Step (M.I.N.S.) for each goal, so your goal transforms into an action. And remember, when it comes to M.I.N.S., be specific.

GOAL #1 _____

Weekly Objective: _____

M.I.N.S. _____

GOAL #2 _____

Weekly Objective: _____

M.I.N.S. _____

GOAL #3 _____

Weekly Objective: _____

M.I.N.S. _____

I can consider today a "win" if I...

This is your #1 Most Important Thing!

TODAY'S TIME-BLOCKING ACTIVITIES

High-achievers know that what gets scheduled gets done. Take a few minutes to think about your goals, your M.I.N.S., and schedule your day. Don't forget to include several breaks.

5:00 _____	11:00 _____	5:00 _____
5:30 _____	11:30 _____	5:30 _____
6:00 _____	12:00 _____	6:00 _____
6:30 _____	12:30 _____	6:30 _____
7:00 _____	1:00 _____	7:00 _____
7:30 _____	1:30 _____	7:30 _____
8:00 _____	2:00 _____	8:00 _____
8:30 _____	2:30 _____	8:30 _____
9:00 _____	3:00 _____	9:00 _____
9:30 _____	3:30 _____	9:30 _____
10:00 _____	4:00 _____	10:00 _____
10:30 _____	4:30 _____	10:30 _____

☐ Did I include enough breaks in the day?

☐ Did I schedule my #1 Most Important Thing?

EVENING REVIEW

Did you accomplish your #1 Most Important Thing today?   Yes ☐   No ☐

Today was awesome because _____

_____

Today I struggled with _____

_____

On a scale of 1–10, with 10 being the highest, I would rate today's productivity at a _____

Tomorrow I will...   Notes

_____   _____

_____   _____

_____   _____

DAILY ACTION PLAN

MORNING ROUTINE

Hours Slept _____   Wake-up Time _____

Water ☐   Daily Journal ☐   _____ ☐   _____ ☐

This morning, I'm grateful for _____

GOALS AND M.I.N.S.

Goals are important to review daily, reinforcing your objectives to your conscious and subconscious mind. But goals alone are not enough. It's also vital that you take time to identify your Most Important Next Step (M.I.N.S.) for each goal, so your goal transforms into an action. And remember, when it comes to M.I.N.S., be specific.

GOAL #1 _____

Weekly Objective: _____

M.I.N.S. _____

GOAL #2 _____

Weekly Objective: _____

M.I.N.S. _____

GOAL #3 _____

Weekly Objective: _____

M.I.N.S. _____

I can consider today a "win" if I...

This is your #1 Most Important Thing!

TODAY'S TIME-BLOCKING ACTIVITIES

High-achievers know that what gets scheduled gets done. Take a few minutes to think about your goals, your M.I.N.S., and schedule your day. Don't forget to include several breaks.

5:00 _____	11:00 _____	5:00 _____
5:30 _____	11:30 _____	5:30 _____
6:00 _____	12:00 _____	6:00 _____
6:30 _____	12:30 _____	6:30 _____
7:00 _____	1:00 _____	7:00 _____
7:30 _____	1:30 _____	7:30 _____
8:00 _____	2:00 _____	8:00 _____
8:30 _____	2:30 _____	8:30 _____
9:00 _____	3:00 _____	9:00 _____
9:30 _____	3:30 _____	9:30 _____
10:00 _____	4:00 _____	10:00 _____
10:30 _____	4:30 _____	10:30 _____

☐ Did I include enough breaks in the day?

☐ Did I schedule my #1 Most Important Thing?

EVENING REVIEW

Did you accomplish your #1 Most Important Thing today?   Yes ☐   No ☐

Today was awesome because _____

_____

Today I struggled with _____

_____

On a scale of 1–10, with 10 being the highest, I would rate today's productivity at a _____

Tomorrow I will...   Notes

_____   _____

_____   _____

_____   _____

DAILY ACTION PLAN
MORNING ROUTINE

Hours Slept _____ Wake-up Time _____

Water ☐   Daily Journal ☐   _____ ☐   _____ ☐

This morning, I'm grateful for _____

GOALS AND M.I.N.S.

Goals are important to review daily, reinforcing your objectives to your conscious and subconscious mind. But goals alone are not enough. It's also vital that you take time to identify your Most Important Next Step (M.I.N.S.) for each goal, so your goal transforms into an action. And remember, when it comes to M.I.N.S., be specific.

GOAL #1 _____

Weekly Objective: _____

M.I.N.S. _____

GOAL #2 _____

Weekly Objective: _____

M.I.N.S. _____

GOAL #3 _____

Weekly Objective: _____

M.I.N.S. _____

I can consider today a "win" if I...

This is your #1 Most Important Thing!

TODAY'S TIME-BLOCKING ACTIVITIES

High-achievers know that what gets scheduled gets done. Take a few minutes to think about your goals, your M.I.N.S., and schedule your day. Don't forget to include several breaks.

5:00 _____	11:00 _____	5:00 _____
5:30 _____	11:30 _____	5:30 _____
6:00 _____	12:00 _____	6:00 _____
6:30 _____	12:30 _____	6:30 _____
7:00 _____	1:00 _____	7:00 _____
7:30 _____	1:30 _____	7:30 _____
8:00 _____	2:00 _____	8:00 _____
8:30 _____	2:30 _____	8:30 _____
9:00 _____	3:00 _____	9:00 _____
9:30 _____	3:30 _____	9:30 _____
10:00 _____	4:00 _____	10:00 _____
10:30 _____	4:30 _____	10:30 _____

☐ Did I include enough breaks in the day?

☐ Did I schedule my #1 Most Important Thing?

EVENING REVIEW

Did you accomplish your #1 Most Important Thing today?   Yes ☐   No ☐

Today was awesome because _____

_____

Today I struggled with _____

_____

On a scale of 1–10, with 10 being the highest, I would rate today's productivity at a _____

Tomorrow I will...   Notes

_____   _____

_____   _____

_____   _____

DAILY ACTION PLAN
MORNING ROUTINE

Hours Slept _____ Wake-up Time _____

Water ☐ Daily Journal ☐ _____ ☐ _____ ☐

This morning, I'm grateful for _____

GOALS AND M.I.N.S.

Goals are important to review daily, reinforcing your objectives to your conscious and subconscious mind. But goals alone are not enough. It's also vital that you take time to identify your Most Important Next Step (M.I.N.S.) for each goal, so your goal transforms into an action. And remember, when it comes to M.I.N.S., be specific.

GOAL #1 _____

Weekly Objective: _____

M.I.N.S. _____

GOAL #2 _____

Weekly Objective: _____

M.I.N.S. _____

GOAL #3 _____

Weekly Objective: _____

M.I.N.S. _____

I can consider today a "win" if I...

This is your #1 Most Important Thing!

TODAY'S TIME-BLOCKING ACTIVITIES

High-achievers know that what gets scheduled gets done. Take a few minutes to think about your goals, your M.I.N.S., and schedule your day. Don't forget to include several breaks.

5:00 _____	11:00 _____	5:00 _____
5:30 _____	11:30 _____	5:30 _____
6:00 _____	12:00 _____	6:00 _____
6:30 _____	12:30 _____	6:30 _____
7:00 _____	1:00 _____	7:00 _____
7:30 _____	1:30 _____	7:30 _____
8:00 _____	2:00 _____	8:00 _____
8:30 _____	2:30 _____	8:30 _____
9:00 _____	3:00 _____	9:00 _____
9:30 _____	3:30 _____	9:30 _____
10:00 _____	4:00 _____	10:00 _____
10:30 _____	4:30 _____	10:30 _____

☐ Did I include enough breaks in the day?　　　☐ Did I schedule my #1 Most Important Thing?

EVENING REVIEW

Did you accomplish your #1 Most Important Thing today?　Yes ☐　No ☐

Today was awesome because _____

_____

Today I struggled with _____

_____

On a scale of 1–10, with 10 being the highest, I would rate today's productivity at a _____

Tomorrow I will...　　　　　　　　　Notes

_____	_____

_____	_____

_____	_____

DAILY ACTION PLAN
MORNING ROUTINE

Hours Slept _____   Wake-up Time _____

Water ☐   Daily Journal ☐   _____ ☐   _____ ☐

This morning, I'm grateful for _____

GOALS AND M.I.N.S.

Goals are important to review daily, reinforcing your objectives to your conscious and subconscious mind. But goals alone are not enough. It's also vital that you take time to identify your Most Important Next Step (M.I.N.S.) for each goal, so your goal transforms into an action. And remember, when it comes to M.I.N.S., be specific.

GOAL #1 _____

Weekly Objective: _____

M.I.N.S. _____

GOAL #2 _____

Weekly Objective: _____

M.I.N.S. _____

GOAL #3 _____

Weekly Objective: _____

M.I.N.S. _____

I can consider today a "win" if I...

This is your #1 Most Important Thing!

TODAY'S TIME-BLOCKING ACTIVITIES

High-achievers know that what gets scheduled gets done. Take a few minutes to think about your goals, your M.I.N.S., and schedule your day. Don't forget to include several breaks.

5:00 _____	11:00 _____	5:00 _____
5:30 _____	11:30 _____	5:30 _____
6:00 _____	12:00 _____	6:00 _____
6:30 _____	12:30 _____	6:30 _____
7:00 _____	1:00 _____	7:00 _____
7:30 _____	1:30 _____	7:30 _____
8:00 _____	2:00 _____	8:00 _____
8:30 _____	2:30 _____	8:30 _____
9:00 _____	3:00 _____	9:00 _____
9:30 _____	3:30 _____	9:30 _____
10:00 _____	4:00 _____	10:00 _____
10:30 _____	4:30 _____	10:30 _____

☐ Did I include enough breaks in the day?   ☐ Did I schedule my #1 Most Important Thing?

EVENING REVIEW

Did you accomplish your #1 Most Important Thing today?   Yes ☐   No ☐

Today was awesome because _____

_____

Today I struggled with _____

_____

On a scale of 1–10, with 10 being the highest, I would rate today's productivity at a _____

Tomorrow I will...   Notes

_____   _____

_____   _____

_____   _____

DAILY ACTION PLAN

MORNING ROUTINE

Hours Slept _____ Wake-up Time _____

Water ☐ Daily Journal ☐ _____ ☐ _____ ☐

This morning, I'm grateful for _____

GOALS AND M.I.N.S.

Goals are important to review daily, reinforcing your objectives to your conscious and subconscious mind. But goals alone are not enough. It's also vital that you take time to identify your Most Important Next Step (M.I.N.S.) for each goal, so your goal transforms into an action. And remember, when it comes to M.I.N.S., be specific.

GOAL #1 _____

Weekly Objective: _____

M.I.N.S. _____

GOAL #2 _____

Weekly Objective: _____

M.I.N.S. _____

GOAL #3 _____

Weekly Objective: _____

M.I.N.S. _____

I can consider today a "win" if I...

This is your #1 Most Important Thing!

TODAY'S TIME-BLOCKING ACTIVITIES

High-achievers know that what gets scheduled gets done. Take a few minutes to think about your goals, your M.I.N.S., and schedule your day. Don't forget to include several breaks.

5:00 _____	11:00 _____	5:00 _____
5:30 _____	11:30 _____	5:30 _____
6:00 _____	12:00 _____	6:00 _____
6:30 _____	12:30 _____	6:30 _____
7:00 _____	1:00 _____	7:00 _____
7:30 _____	1:30 _____	7:30 _____
8:00 _____	2:00 _____	8:00 _____
8:30 _____	2:30 _____	8:30 _____
9:00 _____	3:00 _____	9:00 _____
9:30 _____	3:30 _____	9:30 _____
10:00 _____	4:00 _____	10:00 _____
10:30 _____	4:30 _____	10:30 _____

☐ Did I include enough breaks in the day?   ☐ Did I schedule my #1 Most Important Thing?

EVENING REVIEW

Did you accomplish your #1 Most Important Thing today?   Yes ☐   No ☐

Today was awesome because _____

_____

Today I struggled with _____

_____

On a scale of 1–10, with 10 being the highest, I would rate today's productivity at a _____

Tomorrow I will...   Notes

_____   _____

_____   _____

_____   _____

DAILY ACTION PLAN
MORNING ROUTINE

Hours Slept _____   Wake-up Time _____

Water ☐   Daily Journal ☐   _____ ☐   _____ ☐

This morning, I'm grateful for _____

GOALS AND M.I.N.S.

Goals are important to review daily, reinforcing your objectives to your conscious and subconscious mind. But goals alone are not enough. It's also vital that you take time to identify your Most Important Next Step (M.I.N.S.) for each goal, so your goal transforms into an action. And remember, when it comes to M.I.N.S., be specific.

GOAL #1 _____

Weekly Objective: _____

M.I.N.S. _____

GOAL #2 _____

Weekly Objective: _____

M.I.N.S. _____

GOAL #3 _____

Weekly Objective: _____

M.I.N.S. _____

I can consider today a "win" if I...

This is your #1 Most Important Thing!

TODAY'S TIME-BLOCKING ACTIVITIES

High-achievers know that what gets scheduled gets done. Take a few minutes to think about your goals, your M.I.N.S., and schedule your day. Don't forget to include several breaks.

5:00 _____	11:00 _____	5:00 _____
5:30 _____	11:30 _____	5:30 _____
6:00 _____	12:00 _____	6:00 _____
6:30 _____	12:30 _____	6:30 _____
7:00 _____	1:00 _____	7:00 _____
7:30 _____	1:30 _____	7:30 _____
8:00 _____	2:00 _____	8:00 _____
8:30 _____	2:30 _____	8:30 _____
9:00 _____	3:00 _____	9:00 _____
9:30 _____	3:30 _____	9:30 _____
10:00 _____	4:00 _____	10:00 _____
10:30 _____	4:30 _____	10:30 _____

☐ Did I include enough breaks in the day?

☐ Did I schedule my #1 Most Important Thing?

EVENING REVIEW

Did you accomplish your #1 Most Important Thing today? Yes ☐ No ☐

Today was awesome because _____

_____

Today I struggled with _____

_____

On a scale of 1–10, with 10 being the highest, I would rate today's productivity at a _____

Tomorrow I will...   Notes

_____   _____

_____   _____

_____   _____

DAILY ACTION PLAN
MORNING ROUTINE

Hours Slept _____   Wake-up Time _____

Water ☐   Daily Journal ☐   _____ ☐   _____ ☐

This morning, I'm grateful for _____

GOALS AND M.I.N.S.

Goals are important to review daily, reinforcing your objectives to your conscious and subconscious mind. But goals alone are not enough. It's also vital that you take time to identify your Most Important Next Step (M.I.N.S.) for each goal, so your goal transforms into an action. And remember, when it comes to M.I.N.S., be specific.

GOAL #1 _____

Weekly Objective: _____

M.I.N.S. _____

GOAL #2 _____

Weekly Objective: _____

M.I.N.S. _____

GOAL #3 _____

Weekly Objective: _____

M.I.N.S. _____

I can consider today a "win" if I...

This is your #1 Most Important Thing!

TODAY'S TIME-BLOCKING ACTIVITIES

High-achievers know that what gets scheduled gets done. Take a few minutes to think about your goals, your M.I.N.S., and schedule your day. Don't forget to include several breaks.

5:00 _____	11:00 _____	5:00 _____
5:30 _____	11:30 _____	5:30 _____
6:00 _____	12:00 _____	6:00 _____
6:30 _____	12:30 _____	6:30 _____
7:00 _____	1:00 _____	7:00 _____
7:30 _____	1:30 _____	7:30 _____
8:00 _____	2:00 _____	8:00 _____
8:30 _____	2:30 _____	8:30 _____
9:00 _____	3:00 _____	9:00 _____
9:30 _____	3:30 _____	9:30 _____
10:00 _____	4:00 _____	10:00 _____
10:30 _____	4:30 _____	10:30 _____

☐ Did I include enough breaks in the day?

☐ Did I schedule my #1 Most Important Thing?

EVENING REVIEW

Did you accomplish your #1 Most Important Thing today?   Yes ☐   No ☐

Today was awesome because _____

_____

Today I struggled with _____

_____

On a scale of 1–10, with 10 being the highest, I would rate today's productivity at a _____

Tomorrow I will...

_____

_____

_____

Notes

_____

_____

_____

DAILY ACTION PLAN
MORNING ROUTINE

Hours Slept _____ Wake-up Time _____

Water ☐ Daily Journal ☐ _____ ☐ _____ ☐

This morning, I'm grateful for _____

GOALS AND M.I.N.S.

Goals are important to review daily, reinforcing your objectives to your conscious and subconscious mind. But goals alone are not enough. It's also vital that you take time to identify your Most Important Next Step (M.I.N.S.) for each goal, so your goal transforms into an action. And remember, when it comes to M.I.N.S., be specific.

GOAL #1 _____

Weekly Objective: _____

M.I.N.S. _____

GOAL #2 _____

Weekly Objective: _____

M.I.N.S. _____

GOAL #3 _____

Weekly Objective: _____

M.I.N.S. _____

I can consider today a "win" if I...

This is your #1 Most Important Thing!

TODAY'S TIME-BLOCKING ACTIVITIES

High-achievers know that what gets scheduled gets done. Take a few minutes to think about your goals, your M.I.N.S., and schedule your day. Don't forget to include several breaks.

5:00 _____	11:00 _____	5:00 _____
5:30 _____	11:30 _____	5:30 _____
6:00 _____	12:00 _____	6:00 _____
6:30 _____	12:30 _____	6:30 _____
7:00 _____	1:00 _____	7:00 _____
7:30 _____	1:30 _____	7:30 _____
8:00 _____	2:00 _____	8:00 _____
8:30 _____	2:30 _____	8:30 _____
9:00 _____	3:00 _____	9:00 _____
9:30 _____	3:30 _____	9:30 _____
10:00 _____	4:00 _____	10:00 _____
10:30 _____	4:30 _____	10:30 _____

☐ Did I include enough breaks in the day?   ☐ Did I schedule my #1 Most Important Thing?

EVENING REVIEW

Did you accomplish your #1 Most Important Thing today?   Yes ☐   No ☐

Today was awesome because _____

_____

Today I struggled with _____

_____

On a scale of 1–10, with 10 being the highest, I would rate today's productivity at a _____

Tomorrow I will...   Notes

_____   _____

_____   _____

_____   _____

DAILY ACTION PLAN
MORNING ROUTINE

Hours Slept _____ Wake-up Time _____

Water ☐ Daily Journal ☐ _____ ☐ _____ ☐

This morning, I'm grateful for _____

GOALS AND M.I.N.S.

Goals are important to review daily, reinforcing your objectives to your conscious and subconscious mind. But goals alone are not enough. It's also vital that you take time to identify your Most Important Next Step (M.I.N.S.) for each goal, so your goal transforms into an action. And remember, when it comes to M.I.N.S., be specific.

GOAL #1 _____

Weekly Objective: _____

M.I.N.S. _____

GOAL #2 _____

Weekly Objective: _____

M.I.N.S. _____

GOAL #3 _____

Weekly Objective: _____

M.I.N.S. _____

I can consider today a "win" if I...

This is your #1 Most Important Thing!

TODAY'S TIME-BLOCKING ACTIVITIES

High-achievers know that what gets scheduled gets done. Take a few minutes to think about your goals, your M.I.N.S., and schedule your day. Don't forget to include several breaks.

5:00 _____	11:00 _____	5:00 _____
5:30 _____	11:30 _____	5:30 _____
6:00 _____	12:00 _____	6:00 _____
6:30 _____	12:30 _____	6:30 _____
7:00 _____	1:00 _____	7:00 _____
7:30 _____	1:30 _____	7:30 _____
8:00 _____	2:00 _____	8:00 _____
8:30 _____	2:30 _____	8:30 _____
9:00 _____	3:00 _____	9:00 _____
9:30 _____	3:30 _____	9:30 _____
10:00 _____	4:00 _____	10:00 _____
10:30 _____	4:30 _____	10:30 _____

☐ Did I include enough breaks in the day?

☐ Did I schedule my #1 Most Important Thing?

EVENING REVIEW

Did you accomplish your #1 Most Important Thing today?   Yes ☐   No ☐

Today was awesome because _____

_____

Today I struggled with _____

_____

On a scale of 1–10, with 10 being the highest, I would rate today's productivity at a _____

Tomorrow I will...

Notes

_____   _____

_____   _____

_____   _____

DAILY ACTION PLAN
MORNING ROUTINE

Hours Slept _____   Wake-up Time _____

Water ☐   Daily Journal ☐   _____ ☐   _____ ☐

This morning, I'm grateful for _____

GOALS AND M.I.N.S.

Goals are important to review daily, reinforcing your objectives to your conscious and subconscious mind. But goals alone are not enough. It's also vital that you take time to identify your Most Important Next Step (M.I.N.S.) for each goal, so your goal transforms into an action. And remember, when it comes to M.I.N.S., be specific.

GOAL #1 _____

Weekly Objective: _____

M.I.N.S. _____

GOAL #2 _____

Weekly Objective: _____

M.I.N.S. _____

GOAL #3 _____

Weekly Objective: _____

M.I.N.S. _____

I can consider today a "win" if I...

This is your #1 Most Important Thing!

TODAY'S TIME-BLOCKING ACTIVITIES

High-achievers know that what gets scheduled gets done. Take a few minutes to think about your goals, your M.I.N.S., and schedule your day. Don't forget to include several breaks.

5:00 _____	11:00 _____	5:00 _____
5:30 _____	11:30 _____	5:30 _____
6:00 _____	12:00 _____	6:00 _____
6:30 _____	12:30 _____	6:30 _____
7:00 _____	1:00 _____	7:00 _____
7:30 _____	1:30 _____	7:30 _____
8:00 _____	2:00 _____	8:00 _____
8:30 _____	2:30 _____	8:30 _____
9:00 _____	3:00 _____	9:00 _____
9:30 _____	3:30 _____	9:30 _____
10:00 _____	4:00 _____	10:00 _____
10:30 _____	4:30 _____	10:30 _____

☐ Did I include enough breaks in the day?   ☐ Did I schedule my #1 Most Important Thing?

EVENING REVIEW

Did you accomplish your #1 Most Important Thing today?   Yes ☐   No ☐

Today was awesome because _____

_____

Today I struggled with _____

_____

On a scale of 1–10, with 10 being the highest, I would rate today's productivity at a _____

Tomorrow I will...   Notes

_____   _____

_____   _____

_____   _____

NOTES

NOTES

NOTES

NOTES

NOTES

NOTES

NOTES

NOTES